STUDENT SURVIVAL MANUAL

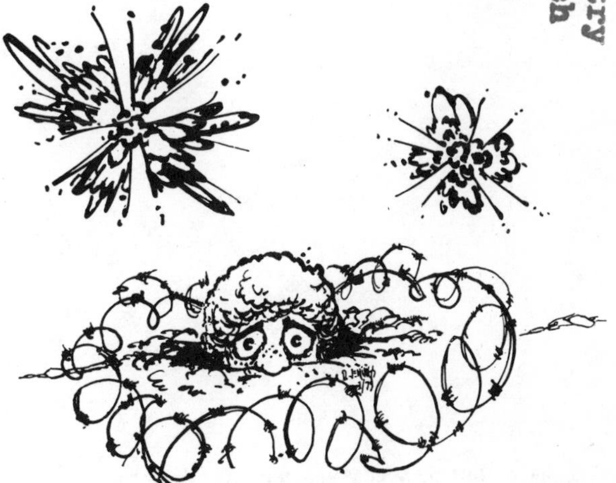

Written and Designed by
RANDY RODDEN

Art by **DOUG JENNINGS**

mott media

Leonard George Goss, Editor
A. G. Smith, Cover Design
Doug Jennings, Art

ISBN 0-915134-85-3

DEDICATION

As a small child, my mother's prayer for me was that as I grew I would be led by wise men. This manual is dedicated to J. R. Sears, Bill Sanders, Chuck Klein, Alan Scholes, and Dad, who have all been used in their own special ways to answer Mom's supplication.

SPECIAL THANKS

. . . to my brother, Dan Rodden, and to Tim Hastings, for their help in initiating this project, and for their wonderful encouragement and counsel.

. . . to Doug Jennings, art director for Student Action for Christ and author of "Luminaus," the monthly comic strip in the newspaper *Issues & Answers,* for his special artistic contribution to the STUDENT SURVIVAL MANUAL.

. . . to Janet Curry, Alicia Jennings, Lee Rodden, Joy Carter, and my gracious wife Leslie, for their many hours of proofreading and typing.

. . . to the youth of this country—their hunger for honest answers has motivated the writing of this book.

STUDENT ACTION FOR CHRIST, INC.

STUDENT SURVIVAL MANUAL was initiated by Student Action for Christ, an interdenominational Christian ministry assisting local churches and Christian organizations in reaching their public schools. Founded in 1972, its goal has been to penetrate the secular campus with the Christian worldview.

Issues & Answers is the SAC monthly newspaper which presents the Christian message to the youth culture. Another SAC publication which seeks to present the Christian perspective in education is *Active Christians in Education,* aimed at parents and teachers.

"The Caleb Campaign" works to have *Issues & Answers* in the hands of every high school student in America, and to provide copies of *Active Christians in Education* for every high school faculty member.

For additional information, call 618-942-7520, or write: Student Action for Christ, P.O. Box 608, Herrin, Illinois 62948.

HOW TO USE THIS MANUAL

the STUDENT SURVIVAL MANUAL . . .

. . . is tailor made for students who want solid answers on the trustworthiness of the Bible without wading through thousands of pages of technical and complex material.

. . . can be used for small or large study groups, classes in church or on campus, or for personal study. It is especially designed as a resource book for students writing research papers or delivering speeches on Christian evidences.

. . . has questions at the end of each chapter to assist readers in meaningful thought and discussion. The questions will also help in self-testing, so the reader will be sure to have understood the essential ideas presented in the chapter. Footnotes are included for those who wish to document the information for classroom use, and the books mentioned at the end of each chapter are suggested for those who would like to pursue the subjects in greater detail.

CONTENTS

SECTION 1

1 / Why Are People Afraid Of It
2 / No Other Book Can Compare
3 / It Can Take It
4 / It's Got Clout

SECTION 2

5 / Under Attack
6 / Makes Good Copy
7 / Doesn't Speak With A Forked Tongue
8 / Three Witnesses From History

SECTION 3

9 / In The Fiery Furnace
10 / The Scrolls That Shut The Mouths of Lions

—HAVE YOU EVER BEEN EMBARRASSED WHEN ONE OF YOUR FRIENDS OR TEACHERS NOTICED YOU CARRYING A BIBLE?

I remember a few years ago while in high school, I finally got the nerve up to carry my Bible to school. I kept it neatly covered by other school materials so that no one would ask me "The Question." But, to my dismay, at lunchtime one of my friends accidentally knocked over my books and what do you think flopped right out in the open for all my friends to see but a big black book with golden letters on the front, spelling, "The Holy Bible."

My heart fell to my feet as one of my friends asked sarcastically what I was doing with a Bible. As my life flashed before me, I remember feeling like the lady in the E. F. Hutton commercial on TV who was sitting in a plush restaurant quietly talking about the stock market. She was asked by a friend what her broker thought about a particular investment. She said, "Well, my broker is E. F. Hutton and E. F. Hutton says . . ." Remember? The whole restaurant stopped dead in their tracks to listen to her answer.

Well, I felt the whole cafeteria had stopped to listen to my answer. I sat there, for what seemed to be an eternity. Finally I flippantly retorted, "Oh, it's for my Bible as Literature course." Luckily, this satisfied their curiosity and things got back to normal as we resumed our daily conversation, which usually centered around the terrible cafeteria food.

Fortunately, no one knew I didn't really have a Bible as Literature course.

Maybe you've experienced a similar situation. I hope you handled it better than I did. If you have felt the need for some solid answers about the Bible, the following material is for you.

You are no longer going to need to be embarrassed about carrying a Bible. In fact, your friends will probably be a little embarrassed that they don't! You see, the Bible is recognized, even by those who reject what it says, as the greatest book ever written! You are going to learn about some of its impressive credentials.

WHY IS THE BIBLE THE MOST ASTONISHING AND OUTSTANDING BOOK OF HISTORY?

FIRST: BECAUSE THE BIBLE HAS HAD AN ASTONISHING INFLUENCE ON GREAT MEN OF HISTORY.

IT'S ASTONISHING!

THE BIBLE'S INFLUENCE ON COLUMBUS

- What do you think motivated Christopher Columbus to sail dangerous, uncharted waters to another land that he had never seen?

- Was it for gold and glory as some historians say?

A. Author Robert Flood has helped us answer this question when he said, "Even secular historians acknowledge that Columbus was a devout man with a sense of destiny. But for the most part they have missed or underplayed the greatest single driving force behind the voyage of Columbus: the impact of the Bible upon his life."[1]

B. Researcher August J. Kling has added, "Columbus' use of the Bible is one of the best documented facts of his remarkable career, but it is one of the least known to the general public . . . . All of Columbus' sailing journals and most of his private letters give evidence of his biblical knowledge and his devout love for Jesus Christ."[2]

Let Columbus Speak for Himself

Columbus tells us in his own words what motivated him to come to the new world. Columbus said, "It was the Lord who put into my mind (I could feel His hand upon me) to sail from here to the Indies . . . . There is no question that the inspiration was from the Holy Spirit, because he comforted me with rays of marvelous illumination from the Holy Scriptures . . . encouraging me continually to press forward, and without ceasing for a moment they now encourage me to make haste . . . . The fact that the gospel must still be preached to so many lands in such a short time—this is what convinces me."[3]

1/5

II. THE BIBLE'S INFLUENCE ON LINCOLN

- Where do you think Lincoln's phrase, "Government of the people, by the people, and for the people," came from?

A. It comes from the introduction to the Wycliffe Bible—the first English version of the Bible. Wycliffe's preface to that translation says, "The Bible will make possible a government of people, by people, and for people."[4]

B. Lincoln also has said, "I believe the Bible is the best gift God has ever given to man. All the good from the Savior of the world is communicated to us through this Book."[5]

III. THE BIBLE'S INFLUENCE ON SIR ISAAC NEWTON

Newton, English scientist and mathematician, who is recognized as one of the greatest figures in the entire history of science, has said, "There are more sure marks of authenticity in the Bible than in any profane [secular] history."[6]

IV. THE BIBLE'S INFLUENCE ON ROBERT E. LEE

The famous general of the Civil War, Robert E. Lee, has expressed the importance of the Bible in his life when he says, "In all my perplexities and distresses, the Bible has never failed to give me light and strength."[7]

V. THE BIBLE'S INFLUENCE ON DANIEL WEBSTER

Daniel Webster attributes his success as a statesman, lawyer and public speaker to the influence of the Bible on his early life. He says, "If there is anything in my thoughts or style to commend, the credit is due to my parents for instilling in me an early love for the Scriptures."[8]

VI. THE BIBLE'S INFLUENCE ON PRESIDENT THEODORE ROOSEVELT

"Every thinking man, when he thinks, realizes that the teachings of the Bible are so interwoven and entwined with our whole civic and social life that it would be literally—I do not mean figuratively, but literally—impossible for us to figure what that loss would be if these teachings were removed."[9]

VII. THE BIBLE'S INFLUENCE ON ITS ENEMIES

- Antagonists to the Bible have recognized the world-transforming power of its message!

EVEN ATHEISTS ARE IMPRESSED!

A. Noted German scientist and philosopher, Ernst Haeckel, was a well-known atheist who rejected the authority of the Bible. He had to admit, however, that "Beyond all doubt the present degree of human culture owes, in great part, its perfection to the propogation of the Christian system of morals and its ennobling influence."[10]

B. Another antagonist of Christianity was Goethe, the German poet who admitted: "the human mind, no matter how far it may advance in every other department, will never transcend the height and moral culture of Christianity as it shines in the Gospels."[11]

C. One of the greatest writers of the 19th century was James Russell Lowell. Though not an evangelical Christian, he recognized the beneficial influence that the skeptics, who hated the Bible, were reaping from its influence. He wrote, "The worst kind of religion is no religion at all, and these men living in ease and luxury, indulging themselves in the amusement of going without religion, may be thankful that they live in lands where the gospel they neglect has tamed the beastliness and ferocity of the men who, *but for Christianity,* might long ago have eaten their carcasses like the South Sea Islanders, or cut off their heads and tanned their hides like the monsters of the French Revolution."[12]

THINK ABOUT IT...

The above comments by Lowell were written about one hundred years ago and are predictive of our times. As mankind has turned away from the Bible man has become more brutal; as schools have rejected the Bible students have become more violent.

D. Immanuel Kant, the famous German philosopher, who certainly was no Bible-believing Christian, has this to say about the Bible: "The existence of the Bible as a book for people, is the greatest benefit which the human race has ever experienced. Every attempt to belittle it is a crime against humanity."[13]

The Bible's influence on great men of history, both believers and unbelievers, is truly astonishing. Think about all the people who have drawn courage, comfort and light from its pages over the centuries. What would the world be like without the Bible???

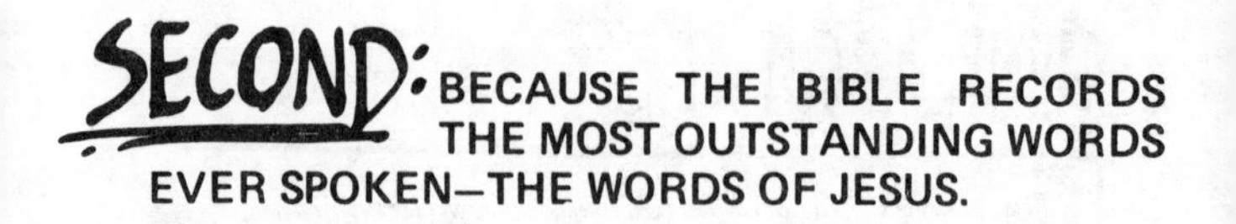

SECOND: BECAUSE THE BIBLE RECORDS THE MOST OUTSTANDING WORDS EVER SPOKEN—THE WORDS OF JESUS.

IT'S OUTSTANDING!

I. THE BIBLE RECORDS THE WORDS OF JESUS

"Statistically speaking, the Gospels are the greatest literature ever written. They are read by more people, quoted by more authors, translated into more tongues, represented in more art, set to more music, than any other book or books written, by any man in any century in any land. But the words of Christ are not great on the grounds that they have such a statistical edge over anybody else's words. They are read more, quoted more, and translated more because they are the greatest words ever spoken."[14]

II. JESUS' EXTRAORDINARY CLAIMS

A. A few days before Jesus was crucified He made a prediction that not even Mohammed Ali would make.

> *JESUS SAID, "HEAVEN AND EARTH WILL PASS AWAY, BUT MY WORDS WILL NOT PASS AWAY" (Lk. 21:33).*

This prediction is even more incredible when we remember that when Jesus made this claim He was not as well known as Ali, Wolfman Jack, the Bee Gees, or even your local D.J.

B. As G. F. Maclean has observed, "Never did it seem more improbable that it [Jesus' prediction] should be fulfilled. But as we look across the centuries we see how it has been realized. His words have passed into the law, they have passed into doctrines, they have passed into proverbs, they have passed into consolations, but they have *never* 'passed away.' What human teacher ever dared to claim an eternity for his words?"[15]

III. JESUS' FRIENDS WERE AMAZED AT HIS WORDS

Luke 4:32 tells us that the disciples "were continually amazed at His teaching."

IV. JESUS' ENEMIES WERE ALSO AMAZED AT HIS WORDS

The only excuse the Jewish guard had for failing to arrest Jesus, as the Pharisees had requested, was, "Never did a man speak the way this man speaks" (John 7:46).

V. JESUS' WORDS ARE THE GREATEST WORDS EVER SPOKEN

A. Joseph Parker has said, "After reading the doctrines of Plato, Socrates or Aristotle, we feel the specific difference between their words and Christ's is the difference between an inquiry and a revelation."[16]

B. Even Sholem Ash admitted, "Jesus Christ is the outstanding personality of all time . . . No other teacher—Jewish, Christian, Buddhist, Mohammedan—is *still* a teacher whose teaching is such a guidepost for the world we live in. Other teachers may have something basic for an Oriental, an Arab, or an Occidental; but every act and word of Jesus has value for all of us. He became the Light of the World. Why shouldn't I, a Jew, be proud of that?"[17]

WORDS of REVOLUTION!

"NO REVOLUTION THAT HAS EVER TAKEN PLACE IN SOCIETY CAN BE COMPARED TO THAT WHICH HAS BEEN PRODUCED BY THE WORDS OF JESUS CHRIST."[18]

—Mark Hopkins

WE HAVE DISCOVERED THAT THE BIBLE HAS HAD AN ASTONISHING INFLUENCE ON GREAT MEN OF HISTORY AND THAT IT RECORDS THE MOST OUTSTANDING WORDS EVER SPOKEN—THE WORDS OF JESUS.

1. Who are some of the great men of history who have been influenced by the Bible?

____

____

2. What was Columbus' real reason for coming to the New World?

____

____

3. Where did Lincoln get the phrase "Government of the people, by the people and for the people" from?

____

4. Why do you think Jesus' words are recognized as the greatest words ever spoken?

____

____

____

5. What book has had the most revolutionary impact upon people?

____________________ WHY? ____________________

____

____

____

Footnotes

1. Robert Flood, *America, God Shed His Grace on Thee,* Chicago: Moody Press, 1975, p. 29.

2. Ibid.

3. Ibid., pp. 30-31.

4. William R. Bright, *Teacher's Manual for the Ten Basic Steps Toward Christian Maturity,* Arrowhead Springs, CA: Campus Crusade for Christ, 1965, p. 5.

5. *Ten Basic Steps Toward Christian Maturity,* Arrowhead Springs, CA: Campus Crusade for Christ, Step 5, 1968, p. 5.

6. Ibid.

7. Ibid.

8. Ibid.

9. Wilbur M. Smith, *Therefore Stand,* Grand Rapids, Michigan: Baker Book House, 1945, p. 28.

10. Bright, op. cit., p. 35.

11. Josh McDowell, *Evidence That Demands A Verdict,* Arrowhead Springs, CA: Campus Crusade for Christ, 1972, p. 33.

12. Smith, op. cit., p. 32.

13. *Ten Basic Steps Toward Christian Maturity,* op. cit.

14. Bernard Ramm, *Protestant Christian Evidence,* Chicago: Moody Press, 1957, p. 170.

15. G. F. Maclean, *Cambridge Bible for Schools, St. Mark,* London: Cambridge University Press, 1893, p. 149.

16. Frank Mead (ed.), *The Encyclopedia of Religious Quotations,* Westwood: Fleming H. Revell, n.d., p. 57.

17. Ibid., p. 49.

18. Ibid., p. 53.

WHY IS THE BIBLE THE MOST REMARKABLE, INCREDIBLE AND AMAZING BOOK OF HISTORY?

FIRST: BECAUSE THE BIBLE IS REMARKABLE IN ITS FORMATION AND UNITY.

IT'S REMARKABLE!

I. THE BIBLE'S VITAL STATISTICS

- Does the following sound like the usual way a book is put together?

THE BIBLE WAS:

A. Written over a 1,600 year time span.

B. Written over 60 generations.

C. Written by 40 plus authors from every walk of life.

- including kings, peasants, philosophers, poets, etc. Moses was a political leader trained in the universities of Egypt; Joshua was a military leader; Daniel was a prime minister; Luke was a doctor; Matthew was a businessman; and Paul was a Rabbi.

D. Written in Different Places.

- Moses in the wilderness, Jeremiah in a dungeon, Daniel in a palace, Luke while traveling.

E. Written in Different Circumstances.

- David during times of war, Solomon during times of peace.

F. Written During Different Moods.

- Some writing from heights of joy and others writing from the depths of sorrow and despair.

G. Written on Three Different Continents.

- Asia, Africa, Europe

H. Written in Three Different Languages.

- **Hebrew** (language of the Old Testament in general), **Aramaic** (small portion of the Old Testament), and **Greek** (language of New Testament).[1]

Dr. Lewis Sperry Chafer has said regarding the formation of the Bible, "The Bible is a collection of sixty-six books which have been written by forty different authors—kings, peasants, philosophers, fishermen, physicians, statesmen, scholars, poets, and plowmen who lived their lives in various countries and experienced no conference or agreement one with another, and over a period of not less than sixteen hundred years of human history."[2]

II. WRITING A BOOK IS DIFFICULT, BUT THIS IS IMPOSSIBLE!

A. Can you imagine trying to write a book with the above characteristics? (Many of the authors had no personal contact with each other.)

B. Can you think of any other book that took 1,600 years to write? (There is none.)

C. How are most books written? (Most books are written by one author, in one generation, in one place, in one mood, in one language on one continent.)

D. What do you think would happen if we tried to go through the past 1,600 years of Western Civilization and put together a book from the literature of that period of history?

- Dysan Hague helps us answer this question when he suggests we "select samples of literature from 1,600 years of Western culture. Take a bit here and a bit there. Bind them together in one volume. What do you get? Nothing but a miscellaneous collection of disconnected fragments."[3] Or as William Orr says, "the most ridiculous, contradictory hodge-podge of nonsense."

- Why a miscellaneous collection of disconnected fragments? (Because everybody has his own personal ideas and opinions; particularly on such controversial subjects as religion, sin, women's rights, Jesus Christ, etc.)

- Think for a moment about trying to find a unanimous opinion on one controversial subject, like sin. Psychologists tell us sin is emotional behavior, philosophers say it's irrational thinking, sociologists say it's cultural lag, Eastern mystics call it bad karma, biologists call it primitive instinct while others deny its existence altogether!

- Or how about women's rights? Just think of the reception Aristotle, Plato or Socrates would receive today if they spoke at an ERA rally. Aristotle said, "Society would be completely disorganized if women were on an equality with their husbands, just as it would be if slaves were on an equality with their masters." Socrates asked his fellow countrymen, "To whom do you talk less than to your wife?" And Plato felt that women should be the common property of men.[4]

the authors of the Bible speak about hundreds of controversial subjects like sin, women's rights, God, racism, heaven and hell, etc., with harmony and agreement.

III. THE BIBLE ACCOMPLISHES THE IMPOSSIBLE

A. Dr. F. F. Bruce, professor of Biblical Criticism at the University of Manchester, England, has said, "The Bible is not simply an anthology [collection of stories, poems, etc.]; there is a **unity which binds the whole together**. An anthology is compiled by an anthologist, but no anthologist compiled the Bible."[5]

B. Another interesting insight into the remarkable formation and unity of the Bible is given by William Orr when he says, **Everything about its [Bible's] composition argues against its unity. There's no reason in the world why it should be one Book. Yet it is, and no honest inquirer will doubt this, if he will take the time to read it carefully."**[6]

> It only makes sense that nothing short of a SUPERNATURAL GOD could produce such a SUPERNATURAL book as the BIBLE.

SECOND: BECAUSE THE BIBLE HAS AN INCREDIBLE TRACK RECORD.

IT'S INCREDIBLE!

I. THE BIBLE IS NUMBER ONE!

- What was the first book ever printed? (the Bible, printed on the Gutenberg press)[7]

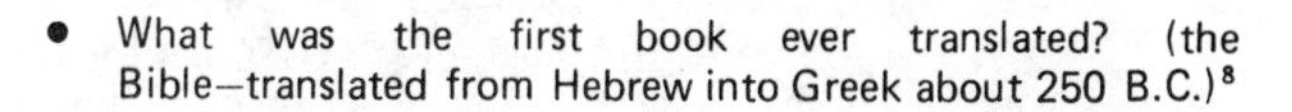

- What was the first book ever translated? (the Bible—translated from Hebrew into Greek about 250 B.C.)[8]

- What book has been translated into more languages than all others? (You're right, the Bible—over 1,100 languages and dialects representing about 90% of the world's population; the closest second is 300 languages.)[9]

- What was the first book read in outer space? (You're right again, the Bible—December 24, 1978, Apollo 8)[10]

- What was the first message sent by Morse code? (Numbers 23:23, "What hath God wrought?")[11]

- What was the longest message ever sent by telegram? (Whole New Testament sent from New York to Chicago)[12]

- What was the highest price ever paid for a book? (ONE MILLION DOLLARS—a Gutenberg Bible)[13]

THE ALL-TIME INTERNATIONAL BEST SELLER...

- What is the number-one best seller of all times? (the Bible—over **TWO BILLION** copies of portions of the Bible).[14] Normally, any book that has been translated into a half-dozen languages and has sold a million copies is recognized as an international best seller.

...EVEN IN NONCHRISTIAN COUNTRIES!

- In the overwhelmingly Buddhist country of Japan, where only one percent of the people claim to be Christian, the Bible ranked as the number-one best seller in 1977! It was reported that at least 1,480,000 copies were sold that year in Japan.

THE BIBLE IS IN DEMAND!

Yes, the Bible was not only the first book printed, first translated, most translated, first read in space, first and longest message given by telegraph, most expensive, but also the number one best seller of all times. **THERE ISN'T EVEN A CLOSE SECOND!** *In fact, "the distant seconds are books related to or dependent on the Bible, such as* Pilgrim's Progress, The Imitation of Christ, *or the works of William Shakespeare."*[15]

One writer informs us that for the British and Foreign Bible Society (this is just one among hundreds of Bible societies that publish Bibles) to keep up with the demands for Bibles it must publish "1 copy every 3 seconds day and night; 22 copies every minute day and night; 1,369 copies every hour day and night; 32,876 copies every day in the year."[16]

THIRD: BECAUSE THE BIBLE HAS AMAZING HISTORICAL ACCURACY.

IT'S AMAZING!

I. THE BIBLE AND HISTORY

A. What book do you think is the most historically reliable book of ancient history . . . Caesar's Gallic Wars, Plato's Republic, the writings of Aristotle? (You guessed it, the Bible; and there isn't even a close second.)

1. Author Josh McDowell, who has done extensive research on the historical reliability of the Bible, substantiated this claim about the Bible when he wrote, "The Bible compared with other ancient writings, has more manuscript evidence than ten pieces of classical literature combined."[17]

2. Dr. Clark Pinnock, professor of theology at McMaster Divinity College, also confirms this idea when he writes, "There exists no document from the ancient world witnessed by so excellent a set of textual and historical testimonies, and offering so superb an array of historical data on which an intelligent decision may be made. An honest person cannot dismiss a source of this kind. Skepticism regarding the historical credentials of Christianity is based upon an irrational (ie. antisupernatural) bias."[18]

II. THE OLD TESTAMENT AND RELIABILITY

The trustworthiness of the Old Testament is discussed by Dr. Bernard Ramm, professor of systematic theology, when he said, "Jews preserved it [Old Testament] as no other manuscript has ever been preserved. . . . they kept tabs on every letter, syllable, word and paragraph They had special classes of men within their culture whose sole duty was to preserve and transmit these documents with practically perfect fidelity–scribes, lawyers, massoretes. Who ever counted the letters and syllables and words of Plato or Aristotle? Cicero or Seneca?[19]

III. THE NEW TESTAMENT AND RELIABILITY

Historian, theologian and professor of law at the International School of Law in Washington, D.C., Dr. John Warwick Montgomery has said, "to be skeptical of the resultant text of the New Testament books is to allow all of classical antiquity to slip into obscurity, for no documents of the ancient period are as well attested bibliographically as the New Testament."[20]

IV. SHAKESPEARE AND THE BIBLE

John Lea, in *The Greatest Book in the World,* compared the Bible with Shakespeare: "In an article in the *North American Review,* a writer made some interesting comparisons between the writings of Shakespeare and the Scriptures, which show that much greater care must have been bestowed upon the biblical manuscripts than upon other writings even when there was so much more opportunity of preserving the correct text by means of printed copies than when all the copies had to be made by hand. He said, 'It seems strange that the text of Shakespeare, which has been in existence less than two-hundred and eight years, should be far more uncertain than that of the New Testament, now over eighteen centuries old, during nearly fifteen of which it existed only in manuscript . . . . With perhaps a dozen or twenty exceptions, the text of every verse in the New Testament may be said to be so far settled by general consent of scholars, that any dispute as to its readings must relate rather to the interpretation of the words than to any doubts respecting the words themselves. But in every one of Shakespeare's thirty-seven plays there are probably a hundred readings still in dispute, a large portion of which materially affects the meaning of the passages in which they occur.' "[21]

THE BIBLE IS UNIQUE (HAVING NO EQUAL) IN RELATION TO ITS AMAZING HISTORICAL ACCURACY. YOU CAN TRUST IT ABOVE AND BEYOND ANY OTHER ANCIENT DOCUMENT!

1. How many of the Bible's eight "vital statistics" can you name?

____

____

____

2. What are some of the ways the Bible is number one?

____

____

____

3. What is the most historically reliable book of ancient history?

____

Footnotes

1. Josh McDowell, *Evidence That Demands a Verdict,* Arrowhead Springs, Ca.: Campus Crusade for Christ, 1972, p. 18.

2. Lewis Sperry Chafer, *Systematic Theology,* Dallas: Dallas Seminary Press, Vol. 1, 1947, p. 29.

3. Bernard Ramm, *Protestant Christian Evidences,* Chicago: Moody Press, 1957, p. 170.

4. *Ten Basic Steps Toward Christian Maturity, Step 5,* Arrowhead Springs, Ca.: Campus Crusade for Christ, 1968, p 5.

5. F. F. Bruce, *The Books and the Parchments,* Rev. ed., Old Tappan, N.J.: Fleming H. Revell Company, 1963, p. 88.

6. *Ten Basic Steps Toward Christian Maturity, Step 5,* op. cit., p. 4.

7. Ramm, op. cit., p. 227.

8. Merrill F. Unger, *Unger's Bible Dictionary,* Rev. ed., Chicago: Moody Press, 1971, p. 1147.

9. Norman L. Geisler and William E. Nix, *A General Introduction to the Bible,* Chicago: Moody Press, 1968, p. 121.

10. Robert J. Hastings, *Hastings Illustrations,* Nashville, Tenn.: Broadman Press, 1971, p. 13.

11. Ibid.

12. Ramm, op. cit., p. 227.

13. *Time Magazine,* March 13, 1978, p. 87.

14. Geisler, op. cit., p. 121.

15. Ibid., pp. 121-22.

16. Ramm, op. cit., p. 227.

17. McDowell, op. cit., p. 21.

18. Clark Pinnock, *Set Forth Your Case,* Chicago: Moody Press, 1971, p. 85.

19. Ramm, op. cit., pp. 230-231.

20. John Warwick Montgomery, *History and Christianity,* Downers Grove, Ill.: Inter-Varsity Press, 1964, p. 29.

21. McDowell, op. cit., p. 22.

WHY IS THE BIBLE THE MOST UNEQUALED AND INCOMPARABLE BOOK OF HISTORY?

BECAUSE THE BIBLE IS UNEQUALED IN ITS SURVIVAL THROUGH PERSECUTION AND CRITICISM.

IT'S UNEQUALED!

I. WHAT BOOK DO YOU THINK HAS BEEN THE MOST PERSECUTED BOOK OF HISTORY? (THE BIBLE)

- The Bible "has been banned, burned, and outlawed from the days of the Roman emperors to present-day Communist dominated countries. But here again, all efforts to stamp out the Bible have been unsuccessful. *No other book has been so persecuted; no other book has been so victorious over its persecutions.*"[1]

EXAMPLES OF THOSE WHO TRIED TO BURN THE BIBLE AND GOT BURNED.

A. One Roman emperor who tried to destroy the Bible was Diocletian. "In A.D. 303 Diocletian issued an edict to destroy Christians and their sacred book: . . . an imperial letter was everywhere promulgated [proclaimed formally] ordering the razing of the churches to the ground and the destruction by fire of the Scriptures."

But Who Got Burned?

- "The historical irony of the above edict to destroy the Bible is that Constantine, the emperor following Diocletian, 25 years later commissioned Eusebius to prepare 50 copies of the Scriptures at the expense of the government."[2]

B. Another famous man of history who viciously attacked the Bible was Voltaire. Sidney Collett, in his book, *All About the Bible,* has written "Voltaire, the noted French infidel who died in 1778, said that in one hundred years from his time Christianity would be swept away from existence and passed into history. But what has happened? Voltaire has passed into history; while the circulation of the Bible continues to increase in almost all parts of the world, carrying blessing wherever it goes."[3]

Voltaire Was "Burned" In His Own House!

- The irony of Voltaire's boast about the extinction of Christianity and the Bible in one hundred years would almost be funny if it weren't so tragic. Dr. Geisler and Nix point out in their book that "only fifty years after his [Voltaire's] death the Geneva Bible Society used his press and house to produce stacks of Bibles."[4]

C. John Lennon of the Beatles just a few years ago made practically the same boast as Voltaire had made almost two centuries earlier. Lennon was quoted in February of 1966, during an interview with the *London Evening Standard*, saying, "Christianity will go. It will vanish and shrink. I needn't argue about that. I'm right and will be proved right. We're more popular than Jesus Christ now."[5]

John Should have Known Better!

The documentation of this interview was ironically found in a book entitled, *The Beatles Forever*. Ironic because just a few years after John's boast the Beatles broke up and today Christianity and Jesus are more popular than ever.

III. WHAT BOOK DO YOU THINK HAS BEEN THE MOST CRITICISED BOOK OF HISTORY. (THE BIBLE)

"No other book has been so chopped, knived, sifted, scrutinized and vilified. What book on philosophy or religion or psychology or belles lettres *of classical or modern times has been subject to such a mass attack as the Bible? with such venom and skepticism? with such thoroughness and erudition? upon every chapter, line and tenent?"*[6]

IV. CAN THE BIBLE WITHSTAND ALL THIS CRITICISM AND SKEPTICISM?

- H. L. Hastings answered this question when he said, "Infidels with all their assaults, make about as much impression on this book as a man with a tack hammer would on the Pyramids of Egypt. When the French monarch proposed the persecution of the Christians in his dominion, an old statesman and warrior said to him: **'Sire, the Church of God is an anvil that has worn out many hammers.'**

"So the hammers of infidels have been pecking away at this book for ages, but the hammers are worn out, and the anvil still endures. **If this book had not been the book of God, man would have destroyed it long ago.** Emperors and popes, kings and priests, princes and rulers have all tried their hand at it; they die and the book still lives."[7]

"A thousand times over, the death knell of the Bible has been sounded, the funeral procession formed, the inscription cut on the tombstone, and committal read. But somehow the corpse never stays put."[8]

SECOND. BECAUSE THE BIBLE IS INCOMPARABLE TO ALL OTHER RELIGIOUS BOOKS.

IT'S INCOMPARABLE

THE BIBLE AND OTHER RELIGIOUS BOOKS

A. Former Professor of Sanskrit, M. Monier-Williams, was a man who had given his life to the study of Eastern religions. He said in comparing other religious books to the Bible, "Pile them, if you will, on the left side of your study table; but place your own Holy Bible on the right side—all by itself, all alone—and with a wide gap between them. For, . . . there is a gulf between it and the so-called sacred books of the East which severs the one from the other utterly, hopelessly, and forever . . . a veritable gulf which cannot be bridged over by any science of religious thought."[9]

B. The man most responsible for translating Eastern religious writings into the English language was Max Mueller. He gave himself to a lifelong study of Eastern literature and his knowledge of religious writings was second to none. Yet he once said to a friend that he was impressed with the immense superiority of the Bible in comparison with other sacred books.[10]

C. A. Galloway has said, "The Bible as a book stands alone. There never was, nor ever will be, another like it. As there is but one sun to enlighten the world naturally, so there is but one Book to enlighten the world spiritually."[11]

The Bible Has UNIVERSAL Appeal!

"It is a book of universal appeal. Kings and princes have studied it. It has fascinated lawyers and doctors, astronomers and housewives, farmers, and physicists. A never-ending stream of humanity has been born, married, and buried under the sound of Bible-reading. It has become the Book of the Eskimo and the African, the giant Watussi and the tiny pygmies. No other book has such universal appeal—*an appeal to men of all temperaments, all races, all employments, all social standing, all economic means, and all gifts of intelligence."*[12]

1. What do Diocletian, Voltaire and John Lennon of the Beatles have in common?

___

___

2. Why has the Bible been able to withstand so much persecution and criticism?

___

___

3. How does the Bible compare with other religious books?

___

___

Footnotes

1. Bernard Ramm, *Protestant Christian Evidences,* Chicago: Moody Press, 1957, p. 170.

2. Josh McDowell, *Evidence That Demands a Verdict,* Arrowhead Springs, Ca: Campus Crusade for Christ, 1972, p. 23.

3. Sidney Collett, *All About The Bible,* Old Tappan, New Jersey: Fleming H. Revell Co., n.d., p. 63.

4. Norman L. Geisler and William E. Nix, *A General Introduction to the Bible,* Chicago: Moody Press, p. 121.

5. Nicholas Schaffner, *The Beatles Forever,* Harrisburg, Pa: Cameron House, 1977, p. 57.

6. Ramm, op. cit., p. 233.

7. McDowell, op. cit., p. 23.

8. Ramm, op. cit., pp. 232-233.

9. Geisler, op. cit., p. 120.

10. Cleland Boyd McAfee, *The Greatest English Classic,* New York: Harper & Brothers Pub., 1912, p. 277.

11. Clyde Francis Lytle, ed., *Leaves of Gold,* Williamsport, Penn: The Coslett Publishing Co., 1938, p. 44.

12. Ramm, op. cit., p. 241.

4 THE BIBLE: IT'S GOT CLOUT

WHY IS THE BIBLE THE MOST EXCEPTIONAL BOOK OF HISTORY?

BECAUSE IT HAS HAD AN EXCEPTIONAL IMPACT ON WESTERN CIVILIZATION.

IT'S EXCEPTIONAL!

I. THE MOST INFLUENTIAL BOOK OF HISTORY

- What book do you think has had the most revolutionary influence on civilization: *Mein Kampf,* by Hitler; *Origin of the Species,* by Darwin; Plato's *Republic*; or how about *Quotations from Chairman Mao*?

A. Well, Dr. Tiplady, along with many others, says it's the Bible. He asserts, "No other book has ever so completely changed the course of human destiny. In light and power the Bible stands by itself. It borrows from none and gives to all . . . . It is the supreme book of Power."[1]

B. Former professor of law at Yale University and one-time president of the American Bar Association, Justice Simeon E. Baldwin, declared in his Presidential address before the American Historical Association, "It may indeed be safely said that no single cause for the spread of religious liberty, and, by consequence, of civil liberty in modern times, has been so powerful as the circulation of the Bible in all languages."[2]

Can't Teach History Without the Bible!

> *"It is impossible to teach history fairly and fully without a frank recognition of the influence of the Bible. Study the Reformation, the Puritan movement, the Pilgrim journeys, the whole of early American history! We can leave the Bible out only by trifling with the facts."*[3]
>
> *—Dr. Cleland B. McAfee*

II. THE BIBLE'S INFLUENCE ON LITERATURE

- Have you ever thought about the influence the Bible has had on such great literary figures as Browning, Bunyan, Chaucer, Dickens, Emerson, Longfellow, Milton, Poe, Shakespeare, Shelly, Tennyson, Twain, Whitman, Whittier and on and on and on?

A. Dr. Bernard Ramm has said, "Without doubt the Bible has penetrated in our literature more minutely than the powers of the finest penetrating oil."[4] And McAfee notes that "English literature has found more of its material in the Bible than anything else. It has looked there for its characters, its illustrations, its subject-matter."[5]

The Bible in the Public School!?

B. Former president of the National Educational Association, Nicholas Butler, made a strong plea for the reading of the Bible in the public schools. His reasons for reading the Bible were not religious but educational. He, along with many other educators, regards an understanding of the Bible as absolutely necessary for a proper understanding of English literature.[6] Also a recent survey conducted by "Literary Cavalcade" magazine found that college English teachers list the Bible as the number one book students should read before entering college![7]

. . . BECAUSE IT OCCUPIES THE "SUPREME PLACE IN ENGLISH PROSE."

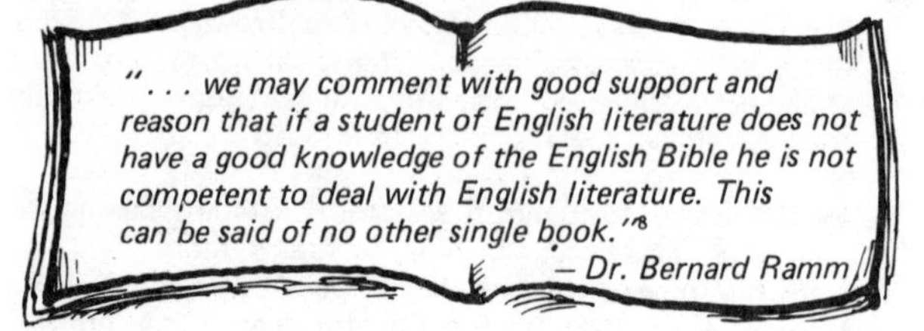

". . . we may comment with good support and reason that if a student of English literature does not have a good knowledge of the English Bible he is not competent to deal with English literature. This can be said of no other single book."[8]

– Dr. Bernard Ramm

ENGLISH STUDENTS BETTER KNOW THE BIBLE . . .

C. Dr. McAfee declares that if we were to "Take any of the great books of literature and black out the phrases which manifestly come directly from the English Bible, . . . you would mark them beyond recovery."

- In fact the Bible's impact on literature has been so great that even if every Bible were destroyed its influence on human life still wouldn't be lost!

But How Could That Be?

- Dr. McAfee answers that question. He says, "If every Bible in any considerable city were destroyed, the Book could be restored in all its essential parts from the quotations on the shelves of the city public library. There are works, covering almost all the great literary writers, devoted especially to showing how much the Bible has influenced them."[9]

III. THE BIBLE'S INFLUENCE ON PUBLIC SPEAKING

- Have you ever noticed how many great speeches contain allusions or direct quotations from the Bible? (For example, in Abraham Lincoln's second inaugural address which only lasted four minutes he quotes in full three Bible verses, and makes reference to two others!)

A. The influence of the Bible on public speaking can be seen by choosing almost any American speaker from Ben Franklin to Martin Luther King; from Thomas Jefferson to John F. Kennedy. Dr. McAfee has said, "Indeed, there is no oratory (public speaking) of our history, . . . which does not feel and show the power of the Scriptures. The English Bible has given our finest eloquence its ideas. its ideals, its illustrations, its phrases."[10]

> *"Whoever has a keen ear in listening to* oratory *will recognize countless references to the Bible. Biblical expressions have become popular speech terms; Biblical characters have become personality types; Biblical stories have provided analogies, illustrations, and themes, world without end!* **No other book—not all books put together—has so entered into the living stream of human speech and oratory as the Bible."**[11] *—Dr. Bernard Ramm*

IV. THE BIBLE'S INFLUENCE ON LAW

- Imagine what it would be like to live in a country where the Ten Commandments were not observed. In fact just the opposite was the law of the land.

- For example maybe some of the laws would be:

THOU SHALT LIE.

THOU SHALT STEAL.

THOU SHALT MURDER!

(What a mess)

A. One doesn't have to be a lawyer or historian to discover that our own country was founded on the belief that man's laws are to be a reflection of God's laws as revealed in the Bible. The founding documents of our country confirm the truth of this idea. For example, check out the Declaration of Independence. Our founding fathers assumed as "self evident, that all men are created equal." Why? Because they believed all men have been created by God! And since all are created by God, all are guaranteed "certain unalienable Rights." In other words, the reason why all men have "Rights" is because those "Rights" are given to all by God.

The principal author of our Declaration of Independence was Thomas Jefferson. He clearly recognized that human rights are a gift of God. He once said, "Can the liberties of a nation be sure when we remove their only firm basis, a conviction in the minds of the people, that these liberties are a gift of God?"[12]

—Thomas Jefferson

B. The Bible's influence on law is not only seen in America but it has filtered into all of Western civilization. As Dr. Ramm has said, "The number of statutes of Biblical origin in the laws of our city, county, state and national government is very large. So much and so long has Biblical jurisprudence [law] filtered into Western culture that most people have long ago lost sight of its origin. The major crimes which Moses legislated against are still major crimes in Western culture. The ideals of the prophets of justice, economic equity, and legal protection of the poor are still the goals of modern jurisprudence.... Moses' distinctions between degrees of crime, for example, manslaughter as less criminal than intentional murder, rape more criminal than fornication, are still active legal principles."[13]

V. THE BIBLE'S INFLUENCE ON POLITICS

- Think about how many forms of government, (from communism to capitalism, from facism to socialism) have tried to justify their causes from the Bible.

A. Dr. Ramm believes that "Almost every form of government has had advocates who presumed to have found Biblical grounds for their theories.... In countless political issues the Bible has been brought in correctly or incorrectly, properly or unceremoniously, to bolster up a case.... in political theory, and around political issues, the Bible has exerted an influence varied and great."[14]

B. Many historians have recognized that our own political system, with its separation of powers, has drawn its life blood from the influence of the Bible upon those who founded our country. As the famous historian H. G. Wells, who was not a Christian, has said: our Constitution is "indubitably [unquestionably] Christian."[15]

VI. THE BIBLE'S INFLUENCE ON GREAT PHILOSOPHERS

- Philosophy is the organized, systematic study of the meaning of life. It has been the pursuit of man throughout history to gain knowledge and insight in order to answer such questions as: Who am I? Where did I come from? Where am I going?

- Did you know that Augustine and Aquinas, who are recognized as two of the greatest philosophers of Western civilization, were both Christians?

A. It has been said that "Augustine bequeathed to the Middle Ages an exceptionally rich Christian and Biblical philosophical heritage" and that "Aquinas' knowledge of the Bible was nothing short of encyclopaedic."[16]

B. History has shown that the Bible has had a profound influence on philosophers. Dr. Ramm has said that such philosophers as Augustine, Aquinas, Descartes, Spinoza, Leibnitz, Locke, Berkeley, Kant and Hume were influenced by the Bible.[17]

VIII. THE BIBLE'S INFLUENCE ON THE ARTS

- Have you ever thought about how many works of art (paintings, statues, buildings, etc.) would be lost if we destroyed all the art that had anything to do with the Bible? Such great artists as Michaelangelo and Rembrandt, as well as many other painters, would be lost without the inspiration they drew from the Bible.

"The galleries of the world are resplendent witness to the Bible's unparalleled influence. In thousands of other buildings, churches, cathedrals, public buildings, private collections, and schools are the numberless objects of Christian art. In the graveyards of the world still further influences of the Bible on art will be found. Some of the greatest artists since classical times have devoted years of their lives, and the best of their efforts, to paint, carve, or sculpture Biblical themes or characters."[18]

- Think about the numerous musical compositions that have drawn their themes directly or indirectly from the Bible. The driving force behind the creative genius of many of history's great musicians has been the Bible.

Some Choir Director!

A. Practically everyone knows that Johanne Sebastian Bach is one of the greatest musicians of history. However, what is seldom known is that Bach was a devout Christian who first played his inspiring compositions in St. Thomas' Church in Germany where he was the organist and choir director. The impact of the Bible upon his life can be seen in his comments on his philosophy of music. He said, "All music should have no other end and aimsthan the glory of God and the soul's refreshment; where this is not remembered there is no real music but only devilish hubub."[19]

Can You "Handel" This?

B. How much poorer Christmas would be without hearing Handel's *Messiah*; recognized as the most popular choral music ever written. But without the Bible's influence on Handel there wouldn't be a Handel's *Messiah*! In fact almost all of Handel's great musical compositions (like *Saul, Esther, Samson, Joshua,* and *Israel in Egypt*) were inspired by Biblical themes or characters.

The "Rolling Stone" Hits Solid Rock

C-We could fill a book with other examples like the above. Even modern day rock stars are not safe from the Bible's influence on their music. Just to cite one recent example, Bob Dylan, who has been called "the greatest singer of our times" by *Rolling Stone Magazine*, has produced what the critics say might be his best album ever. The album is called "Slow Train Coming." It is filled with clear allusions to the Bible!

Something Extra

These first four chapters have presented several reasons why the Bible is recognized as the greatest book of history. One need go no further to establish the fact that the Bible is the most outstanding piece of literature ever produced!

Wouldn't it be great if your friends and teachers knew this? They can! It just may make them think twice the next time they see you carrying your Bible.

Why don't you try it out on your friends. With this information you could write research papers, give speeches, and "be prepared to give an answer to everyone who asks you to give the reason for the hope that you have." (I Peter 3:15) The footnotes and selected books for further study are to help you document this information for your friends and teachers.

1. What book do college English teachers recommend as the most important book to read before entering college?

____

2. Why did the founders of our country believe that all men were created equal?

____

____

3. What are some creative ways to use this "Survival Kit" to witness to your friends?

Some examples: Give one to your friend, use it to write a research paper—Now you think of some ideas.

____

____

____

Footnotes

1. Bernard Ramm, *Protestant Christian Evidences,* Chicago: Moody Press, 1957, p. 233.

2. Wilbur M. Smith, *Therefore Stand,* Grand Rapids, Mich.: Baker Book House, 1945, p. 527.

3. Cleland Boyd McAfee, *The Greatest English Classic,* New York: Harper & Brothers Pub., 1912, p. 282.

4. Ramm, op. cit., p. 235.

5. McAfee, op. cit., r 139.

6. Ibid., p. 285.

7. *Literary Cavalcade* magazine, Vol. 32, No. 2, November 1979, p. 3.

8. Ramm, op. cit., p. 235.

9. McAfee, op. cit., p. 134.

10. Ibid., p. 221.

11. Ramm, op. cit., pp. 235-236.

12. John W. Whitehead, *The Separation Illusion,* Milfred, Mich.: Mott Media, 1977, p. 21.

13. Ramm, op. cit., pp. 236-237.

14. Ibid., p. 237.

15. Whitehead, op. cit., p. 24.

16. Ramm, op. cit., pp. 237-238.

17. Ibid., p. 238.

18. Ibid., p. 239.

19. *Encyclopedia Americana,* Vol. 3, p. 16.

Dig Deeper with These Books

Flood, Robert. *America, God Shed His Grace On Thee.* Chicago: Moody Press, 1975.

McAfee, Cleland Boyd. *The Greatest English Classic.* New York: Harper & Brothers Pub., 1912.

McDowell, Josh. *Evidence That Demands a Verdict.* Arrowhead Springs, CA: Campus Crusade for Christ, 1972.

Pickering, Hy. *One Thousand Wonderful Things About the Bible.* London: Pickering and Ingles, n.d.

Ramm, Bernard. *Protestant Christian Evidences.* Chicago: Moody Press, 1957.

Smith, Wilbur M. *The Incomparable Book.* Minneapolis: Beacon Publications, 1961.

5

THE NEW TESTAMENT: UNDER ATTACK

Thomas Paine almost two hundred years ago said, "When I get through there will not be five Bibles in America."[1] This threat was echoed in his famous essay, "The Age of Reason", in which he presented arguments that he felt would forever destroy Christianity and the Bible.

Shortly after the completion of "The Age of Reason" the French Institute in Paris issued what they believed to be a list of eighty-two errors in the Bible. During this same period, the prestigious University of Tubingen in Germany had rejected the New Testament as a fraud that was produced in the middle of the second century A.D. Others even went so far as to say that Jesus Christ may have never even existed! This skeptical attitude toward the Bible was characteristic of hundreds of philosophers and theologians throughout the eighteenth and nineteenth centuries who spent millions of hours trying to forever lay the Bible in its grave.

• How has the Bible fared after two centuries of intensive skepticism and criticism?

Time magazine, in a cover story on the Bible, answers that question with this conclusion: "After more than two centuries of facing the heaviest scientific guns that could be brought to bear, the Bible has survived—and is perhaps better for the siege. Even on the critics' own terms—historical fact—the Scriptures seem more acceptable now than they did when the rationalists began the attack."[2]

The vicious attacks that have been leveled at the Bible are nothing new. However, what has changed is that, at an increasing rate, the attacks against the Bible are now being mouthed by the uninformed. The last two hundred years of scholarship has confirmed, not destroyed the integrity of the Bible. The last "gun" of the rationalists was silenced as early as 1940 in a book written by one of this century's leading Bible scholars, Sir Frederic Kenyon. He said, "Both the authenticity and the general integrity of the books of the New Testament may be regarded as finally established."[3]

However, don't get the wrong idea. Even though the objections of the critics have been adequately answered and the facts on the reliability of the Bible are in, the battle is not over. The propaganda and prejudices of the past two hundred years cannot be changed overnight. These rationalistic arguments are still being presented as fact in many high school and university classrooms. Christian students and teachers must be prepared to answer these objections to faith.

I. THE NEW TESTAMENT ON TRIAL

A. What would you say if someone said to you:

- You don't really believe in the Bible, do you? You know it's full of errors and contradictions.

OR...

- What if your Bible as Literature teacher told you that scholars agree that the Gospels are not a reliable historical record of the life of Christ since they were not written until a full century after Jesus Christ supposedly lived.

- Have you ever felt like you had to put your brain on the shelf to believe that the Bible was really trustworthy?

- When someone has challenged your belief in the Bible, have you responded with anger and defensiveness because you knew you really didn't have an answer to his question?

- Have you ever felt a little intimidated by the challenges of some non-Christian teacher or professor who throws a lot of fancy terminology at you and then says the magic words: "Scholars agree that the Bible is an inspired book of mythology." Your confidence melts right before his eyes.

B. If you can identify with any of these questions then this section is for you. If you have been afraid that as knowledge increases, the Bible's trustworthiness decreases, then let me give you a word of encouragement. Over the past several centuries the Bible has stood up to the strongest philosophical, religious, literary and scientific criticism that the world could dish out. The Scriptures have only been proven *more* reliable as a result. It is not knowledge but ignorance that is one of the biggest enemies of the Bible.

II. HOW DO WE BEGIN?

- How do we know that the New Testament is an authentic and reliable book which accurately presents first century eye witness testimony of the life and teachings of Jesus Christ? We establish the New Testament's trustworthiness by submitting it to the same scientific tests which are used to test the reliability of any ancient historical document. When historians apply these tests to the New Testament the results confirm what Christians have believed all along—God has preserved through the years an historically reliable Bible.

III. WHAT ARE THE SCIENTIFIC TESTS?

- Dr. Sanders, a leading military historian, lists the basic tests in his book entitled, *Introduction to Research in English Literary History.* These tests are to be applied to all ancient documents alike to determine the documents' reliability. The three tests are: the bibliographic test, the internal evidence test and the external evidence test.

IV. WE DON'T HAVE AN AUTOGRAPHED COPY

A. Before we examine more closely these tests, we must first realize that the reason these tests are important is because the original handwritten letters of the New Testament have perished with time. Scholars call these original letters "autographs." All ancient documents were written on materials that would perish with time. So it is not surprising that the original writings of Caesar, Plato, Herodotus, etc., as well as the original New Testament autographs, no longer exist. What historians are concerned with are the copies that were made from the originals.

I.B.M. - WHERE WERE YOU WHEN WE NEEDED YOU?

B. Remember, during the time of Christ the apostles didn't have a Xerox machine and the printing press wasn't invented until the fifteenth century! Therefore, to keep ancient literature from perishing, these ancient documents had to be copied *by hand* from one generation to the next for hundreds of years.

V. BUT WHY WOULD GOD ALLOW THE ORIGINAL LETTERS OF THE NEW TESTAMENT TO PERISH?

- It does seem at first glance that the easiest way for God to assure us that our Bible records the very words of the apostles would be to preserve the original letters. However, "God's ways are not our ways," and He obviously did not choose to do so. Many Bible scholars feel the reason for this is the tendancy of man to worship religious relics. History has demonstrated this to be true. II Kings 18:4 is a good example. The brazen serpent made by Moses was later worshiped by the Israelites. The Bible makes it unmistakeably clear that we are not to worship (idolize) anything but God. How it must grieve God to see Christians idolize religious relics, buildings, statues, etc. God has been gracious in not allowing us the opportunity to worship the original letters of the Bible.

VI. IF WE DON'T HAVE THE ORIGINAL LETTERS THEN THERE MUST BE MISTAKES IN THE COPIES

A. Human beings do make mistakes and since these documents were copied for hundreds of years, one could expect that there would have been an occasional slip of the pen (not to mention intentional changes), no matter how careful they tried to be.

B. No one today questions the fact that there are mistakes (what scholars call variant readings) in the existing copies of the New Testament. What scholars mean by a variant reading is that a verse in one New Testament copy reads slightly differently than the same verse in another New Testament copy. In fact, there are some 200,000 variant readings in the existing copies of the New Testament.[4]

VII DON'T THESE VARIANT READINGS SHOOT THE BIBLE FULL OF HOLES?

A. Ezra Abbot, a member of the American Revision Committee, asked the above question when he said, "Must not these [variant readings] render the text of the New Testament wholly uncertain, and thus destroy the foundation of our faith?"[5] He answers his own question later with a resounding NO!

FIRST IMPRESSIONS CAN BE WRONG

B. At first these thousands of variant readings may appear to indicate that the Bible is full of errors. But as one studies the facts more carefully, he finds that to say that there are thousands of variant readings in the Bible can be misleading

C. Dr. Norman Geisler, professor of systematic theology at Dallas Theological Seminary, helps clarify this issue when he writes: "There is an ambiguity in saying that there are some 200,000 variants in the existing manuscripts of the New Testament, since these represent only 10,000 places in the New Testament. If one single word is misspelled in 3,000 different manuscripts, this is counted as 3,000 variants or readings. Once this counting procedure is understood, and the mechanical (orthographic) variants have been eliminated, the remaining, significant variants are surprisingly few in number."[6]

VIII. HOW SIGNIFICANT ARE THE 10,000 PLACES WHERE THE VARIANT READINGS OCCUR?

A. To the average Bible reader these variant readings have no significance. So far as you and I would be concerned we would not notice any difference in reading the original of Paul's letters or a good modern version of them.

SCHOLARS AREN'T IMPRESSED

B. B. F. Westcott and F. J. A. Hort, two of the world's leading authorities on New Testament manuscripts, have been quoted by Dr. Geisler as having estimated that, "only about one-sixtieth [of the variant readings] rise above 'trivialities,' or can in any sense be called 'substantial variants.' "[7]

C. Historian Philip Schaff says that only about 50 of the thousands of variant readings are of any real significance. He goes on to state that of the 50 significant variants, not a single one affects "an article of faith or a precept of duty."[8]

BIBLE TRUTH UNAFFECTED

D. Sir Frederic Kenyon, former director and principal librarian of the British Museum, has also said that, "No fundamental doctrine of the Christian faith rests on a disputed reading . . . . It cannot be too strongly asserted that in substance the text of the Bible is certain. Expecially is this the case with the New Testament."[9]

E. Dr. Geisler also refers to Greek scholar A. T. Robertson, who "suggests that a real concern of textual criticism is of a 'thousandth part of the entire text.' This would make the reconstructed text of the New Testament 99.9 percent free from substantial or consequential error. Hence, as Warfield observed, the great mass of the New Testament, in other words, has been transmitted to us with no, or next to no, variations."[11]

F. In summary, the truth about variants in the Bible is that there are amazingly few true variant readings, rather than there being thousands. As Dr. Kenyon says, "It is reassuring at the end to find that the general result of all these discoveries (of manuscripts) and all this study is to strengthen the proof of the authenticity of the Scriptures, and our conviction that we have in our hands, in substantial integrity, the veritable Word of God."[12]

1. What are the three tests that are applied to ancient documents to determine their historical reliability?

______

______

______

2. Why do we not have the original hand-written letters of the Bible?

______

______

______

3. Why would God allow the original hand-written letters of the Bible to perish?

______

______

______

1. John F. MacArthur Jr., *Focus on Fact,* Old Tappan, New Jersey: Fleming H. Revell Company, 1977, p. 65.

2. "The Bible: The Believers Gain", *Time,* December 30, 1974, p. 41.

3. Frederic G. Kenyon, *The Bible and Archaeology,* New York: Harper & Row, 1940, p. 288.

4. Norman L. Geisler and William E. Nix, *A Genera Introduction to the Bible,* Chicago: Moody Press, 1968, p. 361.

5. Josh McDowell, *Evidence That Demands a Verdict,* Arrowhead Springs, California: Campus Crusade for Christ, 1972, p. 43.

6. Geisler, op. cit., p. 361.

7. Ibid., p. 365.

8. Ibid., pp. 365-366.

9. Frederic G. Kenyon, *Our Bible and The Ancient Manuscripts,* New York: Harper and Brothers, 1941, p. 23.

10. Geisler, op. cit., p. 366.

11. Frederic G. Kenyon, *The Story of the Bible,* Grand Rapids, Michigan: William B. Eerdmans Publishing Company, 1967, p. 113.

WHY IS THE NEW TESTAMENT REGARDED AS THE MOST HISTORICALLY RELIABLE BOOK OF ANCIENT HISTORY?

BECAUSE IT HAS MORE DOCUMENTARY EVIDENCE THAN ANY OTHER ANCIENT PIECE OF LITERATURE.

I. THE BIBLIOGRAPHIC TEST

A. This test concerns itself with:

1. The number of existing manuscript copies of the original document.

2. How closely to the original those copies were written.

- Generally speaking, the more copies that exist and the closer these copies were made to the original, the stronger the evidence for the given document's historical reliability.

By comparing the manuscript copies of the New Testament, textual scientists can reconstruct with a high degree of accuracy (99.9%) what the original New Testament said.

DEAR MR. PRESIDENT...

B. An illustration will help clarify this point. Imagine as a class project your English class has decided to write the President of the United States. Much to your surprise, a month later you receive a personal letter of response on official White House stationary from the President. Everyone is excited to get a chance to read the letter.

BUT soon a problem arises. Who gets to keep this valuable letter? After some heated discussion, your class agrees that the school should keep it and the students will make their own hand-written copies. (For the sake of illustration, let's assume there's no such thing as a copy machine.)

CASE OF THE MISSING LETT R

- A few days later a horrible tragedy occurs. Someone breaks into your school and steals a number of valuable items, including the original letter from the President.

Question: How can we ever know what the President said since we no longer have the original letter?

Answer: We have 20 copies of the letter that were made by the English class.

PROBLEM:

However, as we begin to examine the copies we find that there are "variant readings." Jill's copy begins as follows: "Dear students, I was glad to receive your letter. . . ." But Martin's letter reads, "Dear students, I was very glad to receive your letter. . . ." One says "very" and the other does not. This variant reading does not change the meaning of the text and neither do most variant readings in the Bible. But is there some way to know which is correct?

THE MAKING of a TEXTUAL SCIENTIST

- We can reconstruct the original letter of the President by comparing the copies of Jill and Martin with the 18 other copies. In doing this we find that the other 18 read just like Jill's. Therefore, it is reasonable to conclude that Martin has made a mistake and Jill has the accurate reading.

- This illustration demonstrates that not having the original document does not prevent us from reconstructing what the original said from the copies. If one only had two copies and they disagreed it would be very difficult to discover what the original said. But if he had three copies, the third would help us decide. Obviously, the more copies you have the better chance you have of getting back to the original. In essence, this is what textual critics do in reconstructing the original text of the New Testament.

II. HOW DO THE BIBLE COPIES COMPARE WITH OTHER ANCIENT LITERATURE?

- Remember, we do not have the original documents of any of the following writings.

A. Caesar wrote his *Gallic Wars* about 50 B.C. A total number of 10 copies have survived to the present day. These manuscripts were copied at least 1,000 years after his death.[1]

B. The writings of Tacitus, a Roman historian who wrote about 100 A.D., are recognized as an outstanding historical source despite the fact that the oldest copy of his work dates 1,000 years after he wrote, and that we possess only 20 copies of his writings.[2]

C. Aristotle wrote his *Poetics* about 350 B.C. The oldest copy dates from the eleventh century A.D., a full 1,400 years later! There are a total of 5 copies from any one of his works.

D. There are 8 existing copies of the writings of Thucydides which date 1,300 years after the original. The same could be said of Herodotus.[4]

THE NEW TESTAMENT WINS!

E. In the case of the New Testament, the manuscript superiority is overwhelming in comparison. To date, there are over 20,000 copies of portions of the New Testament! The closest second is the *Iliad* which has 643 copies.[5]

- Of the 20,000 copies over 4,000 of these are written in Greek, the language of the original documents. One of the most famous of these Greek manuscripts is Codex Vaticanus. This manuscript contains the whole New Testament and was written less than 300 years after the completion of the last book of the Bible (95 A.D.). We also have copies of portions of the New Testament that take us back to the 2nd century, while the earliest fragment of the New Testament is a portion of the Gospel of John that is dated about 120 A.D.[6]

III. THE NEW TESTAMENT HAD TO BE WRITTEN IN THE FIRST CENTURY.

A. Many scholars used to scoff at the reliability of the New Testament because they said it wasn't written until the middle of the second century, more than one hundred years after Christ lived. This view can no longer be accepted for at least two reasons.

FIRST: The fragment of the Gospel of John that I mentioned earlier is dated about 120 A.D. It would therefore have been copied about a generation after the completion of the original manuscript written by the apostle John in 95 A.D. It is also interesting to note that this fragment was found in Egypt hundreds of miles from Asia Minor where John wrote the original book. The existence of this copy alone destroys the critics' view that the New Testament wasn't written until the middle of the second century. After all, it's impossible to have a copy that predates the original!

SECOND: The second reason why the New Testament had to be written in those few years after the first coming of Christ is discussed by Dr. Miller Burrows of Yale University. Burrows' argument is summarized by Dr. Mounce when he writes, "the study of historical grammar based on archaeological evidence shows that the Greek of the New Testament is first century [not second century] Greek, leading to the conclusion that the New Testament books were written during the first century."[7]

IV THE EVIDENCE SPEAKS FOR ITSELF.

- The facts clearly show that the New Testament is backed up by more manuscript evidence than even the ancient literature that all scholars agree is historically reliable.

A Leading textual scholar Sir Frederic Kenyon has said, "Scholars are satisfied that they possess substantially the true text of the principal Greek and Roman writers whose works have come down to us, of Sophocles, of Thucydides, of Cicero, of Virgil; yet our knowledge of their writings depends on a mere handful of manuscripts, whereas the manuscripts of the New Testament are counted in hundreds, and even thousands."[8]

B. The implication of what Kenyon is saying is stated by New Testament scholar J. Harold Greenlee when he writes, "Since scholars accept as generally trustworthy the writings of the ancient classics . . . it is clear that the reliability of the text of the N.T. is likewise assured."[9]

> *"To be skeptical of the resultant text of the New Testament books is to allow all of classical antiquity to slip into obscurity for no documents of the ancient period are as well attested bibliographically as the New Testament."*[10]
>
> *–Dr. John Warwick Montgomery*

THE POINT IS...

Don't let someone tell you that he accepts the trustworthiness of Aristotle or Plato and yet rejects the reliability of the New Testament–that's dishonest!

1. What are the two parts of the bibliographic test?

____

____

____

2. How many copies of portions of the New Testament exist and what document is the closest second in the number of manuscript copies?

____

____

____

3. What are the two major reasons why the New Testament had to have been written in the first century?

____

____

____

1. Josh McDowell, *Evidence That Demands a Verdict,* Arrowhead Springs, California: Campus Crusade for Christ, 1972, p. 48.

2. Ibid.

3. Ibid.

4. Ibid.

5. Josh McDowell, *More Than a Carpenter,* Wheaton, Illinois: Tyndale House Publishers, Inc., 1977, p. 48.

6. Norman L. Geisler and William E. Nix, *A General Introduction to the Bible,* Chicago: Moody Press, 1968, p. 268.

7. Robert H. Mounce, ed. by Howard F. Vos, *Can I Trust the Bible?* Chicago: Moody Press, 1963, p. 176.

8. Frederic G. Kenyon, *The Bible and Archaeology,* New York: Harper & Row, 1940, p. 29.

9. J. Harold Greenlee, *Introduction to New Testament Textual Criticism,* Grand Rapids, Michigan: Eerdmans Publishing Co., 1964, p. 16.

10. John Warwick Montgomery, *History & Christianity,* Downers Grove, Illinois: InterVarsity Press, 1964, p. 29.

WHY IS THE NEW TESTAMENT REGARDED AS THE MOST HISTORICALLY RELIABLE BOOK OF ANCIENT LITERATURE?

BECAUSE THE NEW TESTAMENT IS INTERNALLY CONSISTENT AND GENUINELY TRUTHFUL.

I. WHERE ARE WE GOING?

- The previous chapter demonstrated the manuscript superiority of the New Testament when compared with other ancient literature. Now we come to the second historical test to see how well the New Testament stacks up.

II. THE INTERNAL TEST—WHAT IS IT?

A. The internal test deals with the document itself. A historian would analyze the document in question to see: (1) How close the author was geographically and chronologically to the events he records; (2) Whether the documents themselves are contradictory or record any known factual inaccuracy; (3) Whether the author has been candid and truthful.

B. The historian proceeds in applying the internal test to a given document with one basic assumption that goes back at least as far as Aristotle. This assumption was stated by Aristotle when he said, "The benefit of the doubt is to be given to the document itself and not arrogated [claimed presumptiously] by the critic to himself."[1] Or, as one modern-day historian has summarized, "One must listen to the claims of the document under analysis and not assume fraud or error unless the author disqualifies himself by contradiction or known factual inaccuracies."[2] In good old American English the document is "innocent until proven guilty."

SOME DON'T PLAY FAIR

C. Ignoring Aristotle's assumption has been one of the greatest mistakes of the skeptics. Their attitude toward the Bible has often times been, "The Bible is guilty until proven innocent." How would you like to be the defendant in a trial like that?

1. An example of this skeptical attitude can be found in the non-believers' attitude toward miracles. They believe that miracles are impossible. Therefore, when they come across a miracle in the Bible they assume it didn't happen. The problem with this attitude is that it rejects them before it ever investigates them. As Dr. Montgomery has said, "The only way we can know if an event can occur is to see whether in fact it has occurred. The problem of 'miracles' then, must be solved in the realm of historical investigation, not in the realm of philosophical speculation."[3]

2. Historian Ethelbert Stauffer has added, "What do we do (as historians) when we experience surprises which run counter to all our expectation, perhaps all our convictions and even our period's whole understanding of truth? We say as one great historian used to say in such instances: 'It is surely possible.' And why not? For the critical historian nothing is impossible."[4]

III. THE INTERNAL TEST AND THE NEW TESTAMENT.

A. How close, geographically and chronologically, were the authors of the New Testament to the events they recorded?

1. The writers claimed to be eyewitnesses.

- Peter said, "For we did not follow cleverly devised tales when we made known to you the power and coming of our Lord Jesus Christ, but we were eyewitnesses of His majesty." (2 Peter 1:16)
- John said, "That which was from the beginning, which we have *heard,* which we have *seen* with our eyes, which we have looked at and our hands have *touched*—this we proclaim concerning the Word of life. The life appeared; we have seen it and testify to it, and we proclaim to you the eternal life [Jesus Christ], which was with the Father and has appeared to us." (I John 1:1-2)

2. The writers claimed to report first-hand information.

- Luke said, "Inasmuch as many have undertaken to compile an account of the things accomplished among us, just as those who from the beginning were eyewitnesses, and servants of the Word have handed them down to us, it seemed fitting for me as well, having investigated everything carefully from the beginning, to write it out for you in consecutive order, most excellent Theophilus, so that you might know the exact truth about the things you have been taught." (Luke 1:1-4)

3. The writers appealed to common knowledge.

- Peter, on the day of Pentecost, said, "Men of Israel, listen to these words: Jesus the Nazarene, a man attested to you by God with miracles and wonders and signs which God performed through Him *in your midst, just as you yourselves know . . .*" (Acts 2:22)

- Paul, before King Festus, made his defense by appealing to common knowledge when he said, "For the king knows about these matters, and I speak to him also with confidence, since I am persuaded that none of these things escape his notice; *for this has not been done in a corner.*" (Acts 26:24-26)

4. The writer's purpose was to record history, not create mythology.

- Luke doesn't start his account of the life of Christ with: "Once upon a time, long ago and far away . . . ." Rather he places the birth of Christ in real history. He says, "Now in the fifteenth year of the reign of Tiberius Caesar when Pontius Pilate was governor of Judea, and Herod was tetrarch of Galilee, and his brother Philip was tetrarch of the region of Ituraea and Trachonitis, and Lysanias was tetrarch of Abilene. . . ." (Luke 3:1) These people really existed!

The New Testament writers were either eyewitnesses or received first-hand information of the events of which they wrote. In other words, they were both geographically and chronologically abreast of the events.

B. Is the New Testament self-contradictory or does it record any factual inaccuracy?

TALK IS CHEAP!

- How many times have you heard, "Well, everybody knows the Bible is full of errors and contradictions." However, as Biblical scholar Robert Mounce says, "To chat about 'contradictions' is one thing; to prove them is something else."[5]

SKEPTICS HAVE BEEN WRONG MORE THAN ONCE

- What many skeptics once thought were contradictions in the Bible have later come to be recognized as only a contradiction in the minds of the skeptics. One such example is cited by Dr. Clark Pinnock. He asserts, "In 1800 the French Institute in Paris issued a list of eighty-two errors in the Bible which they believed would destroy Christianity. Today none of these 'errors' remain! With further reflection and new discoveries, these 'errors' were cleared away. Surely it will be so with all such difficulties. We have our Savior's word for that."[6]

- One of the most intriguing examples of what was once thought by liberal scholars to be an *absolute contradiction* in the Bible was the story of the blind men who were healed near Jericho. Matthew and Mark say that Jesus' healing miracle was performed while leaving Jericho and Luke says the miracle was performed as Jesus was entering Jericho. (Matt. 20:29; Mk. 10:46; Lk. 18:35). Liberal scholars said this was an unquestionable error in the Bible. It certainly does *appear* to be a contradiction!

JERICHO'S CRITICS COME TUMBLIN'

However, what appears to be a slip of the pen by one of the Gospel writers is in fact now recognized as compelling evidence for the truthfulness and candid account of eyewitness testimony. Several years ago, archaeologists dug up the city of Jericho and found that there is an old and new city of Jericho with a plot of land separating the two. Jesus probably performed this miracle while in between old and new Jericho. Therefore, Matthew and Mark could say, from their perspective, that Jesus was leaving Jericho, while Luke said he was entering; and there would be no contradiction. Rather than this being a weakness of the Bible's testimony we find that it actually is a great strength of the Gospel writers' independent testimony.

C. Do the authors appear to be honest and truthworthy?

- Some non-believers have claimed that the authors of the New Testament were not telling the truth, but made the whole story up. This claim is contradicted by several lines of evidence.

A TESTIMONY SIGNED IN BLOOD!

1. First, the critic must show beyond a reasonable doubt that the writers of the New Testament had a reason to lie and were the type of people who would lie. This is extremely difficult to do since about the only thing the disciples gained from their belief was heartache, poverty, estrangement from country, family and friends, as well as death Remember, most of them were tortured and killed for what they wrote. As someone has said, "They signed their testimony in blood!"

2. Second, let's assume for the sake of argument that the disciples had some motive for making up this story of the life of Christ. But is it reasonable to believe that a few simple men could have invented the Person and teachings of Christ even if they had wanted to?

WHICH IS A BIGGER MIRACLE?

- Will Durant, one of history's most prolific chroniclers, has exposed the absurdity of such an idea. He says, "That a few simple men should in one generation have invented so powerful and appealing a personality, so lofty an ethic, and so inspiring a vision of human brotherhood, would be a miracle far more incredible than any recorded in the Gospels. After two centuries of Higher Criticism, the outlines of the life, character, and teaching of Christ remain reasonably clear, and constitute the most fascinating feature in the history of Western man."[7]

> "IT WOULD TAKE MORE THAN A JESUS TO INVENT A JESUS"
>
> —HISTORIAN PHILIP SCHAFF

3. Third, assuming again for the sake of argument that the disciples could have invented the Person of Christ, is it reasonable to believe that the disciples could have gotten others to believe them?

- New Testament scholar Dr. F. F. Bruce shows that it's not easy to make up a good story and then get others to believe it when he writes, "And it can have been by no means so easy as some writers seem to think to invent words and deeds of Jesus in those early years, when so many of His disciples were about who could remember what had and had not happened."[8]

THE DISCIPLES COULDN'T AFFORD TO LIE!

"It was not only friendly eyewitnesses that the early preachers had to reckon with; there were others less well disposed who were also conversant with the main facts of the ministry and death of Jesus. The disciples could not afford to risk inaccuracies (not to speak of wilful manipulation of the facts), which would at once be exposed by those who would be only too glad to do so. On the contrary, one of the strong points in the original apostolic preaching is the confident appeal to the knowledge of the hearers; they not only said, 'We are witnesses of these things,' but also, 'As you yourselves also know' (Acts 2:22). Had there been any tendency to depart from the facts in any material respect, the possible presence of hostile witnesses in the audience would have served as a further corrective."[9]

LIARS DON'T EXPOSE THEIR OWN WEAKNESSES

4. Fourth, the evidence supports the belief that the disciples were honest, straightforward men. They do not manifest the characteristics of someone who is trying to invent, manipulate or conceal the truth. In fact, the brash honesty of these men in openly recording their own weaknesses for the whole world to see is hardly the attitude of deceivers.

- Will Durant alludes to this candid attitude when he writes, "they [N.T. writers] record many incidents that mere inventors would have concealed—the competition of the apostles for high places in the Kingdom, their flight after Jesus' arrest, Peter's denial, the failure of Christ to work miracles in Galilee, the references of some auditors to his possible insanity, his early uncertainty as to his mission, his confessions of ignorance as to the future, his moments of bitterness, his despairing cry on the cross; no one reading these scenes can doubt the reality of the figure behind them."[10]

5. Finally, C. S. Lewis, a former professor of medieval and renaissance literature at Cambridge University who is widely recognized as an authority on literary myth, presents a compelling reason why he rejects the myth hypothesis. Speaking of the life of Jesus recorded in the Gospel of John, Lewis wrote, "there are only two possible views. Either this is reportage or else, some unknown writer in the second century, without known predecessors or successors, suddenly anticipated the whole technique of modern, novelistic, realistic narrative. If it is untrue, it must be narrative of that kind. The reader who doesn't see this has simply not learned to read."[11]

- Lewis' point is simply that if the Gospels are not true history but myth or parable, then the authors wrote a fictional book using the literary technique of the realistic narrative. But that can hardly be possible since the realistic narrative was not used by writers of fiction until modern times. Therefore, Lewis would say that the literary evidence supports the trustworthiness of the Gospel writers.

In summary, the authors of the New Testament were both geographically and chronologically abreast of the recorded events; there are no contradictions or factual inaccuracies in the text; and it can be established beyond a reasonable doubt that the authors were trustworthy. Thus, the New Testament passes the "Internal Test" in magnificent form.

1. What are the three questions that the Internal Test answers?

_______________ _______________

____

____

2. Give one example of what liberal scholars once thought was a contradiction in the Bible, but has now been proven to be historically accurate.

____

____

____

3. Can you list five evidences supporting the truthfulness of the writers of the New Testament?

____

____

____

Footnotes

1. John Warwick Montgomery, *History & Christianity,* Downers Grove, Illinois: InterVarsity Press, 1964, p. 29.

2. Ibid.

3. Ibid., p. 75.

4. Ibid., p. 76.

5. Robert H. Mounce, ed. by Howard F. Vos, *Can I Trust the Bible?,* Chicago: Moody Press, 1963, p. 177.

6. Clark H. Pinnock, *Set Forth Your Case,* Chicago: Moody Press, 1971, pp. 102-103.

7. Will Durant, *Caesar and Christ* in *The Story of Civilization,* Vol. 3, New York: Simon & Schuster, 1944, p. 557.

8. F. F. Bruce, *The New Testament Documents: Are They Reliable?,* Downers Grove, Illinois: InterVarsity Press, 1964, p. 33.

9. Ibid., p. 46.

10. Durant, op. cit., p. 557.

11. C. S. Lewis, *Christian Reflections,* Grand Rapids, Michigan: William B. Eerdmans Publishing Co., 1967, p. 155.

8 THE NEW TESTAMENT: THREE WITNESSES FROM HISTORY

WHY IS THE NEW TESTAMENT REGARDED AS THE MOST HISTORICALLY RELIABLE BOOK OF ANCIENT HISTORY?

NO OTHER ANCIENT BOOK HAS BEEN SUPPORTED BY MORE EVIDENCE FOUND OUTSIDE ITSELF THAN HAS THE NEW TESTAMENT.

I. THE EXTERNAL EVIDENCE TEST

A. The external test is the third and final test applied to ancient documents to determine their reliability. In relation to the New Testament, the external test deals with other relevant historical materials other than the Bible. These other materials are examined to see if they confirm or deny the internal testimony of the New Testament.

B. The external test when applied to the New Testament would consist of an examination of: (1) Early Christian writings, (2) Non-Christian writings, and (3) Archaeology.

II. EARLY CHRISTIAN WRITINGS

- Do early Christian writings support or deny the reliability of the New Testament?

A. Drs. Norman Geisler and William Nix have extensively documented numerous ancient Christian quotations from the New Testament. These quotations date as far back as 70 A.D. and they say that "every book of the New Testament was quoted clearly before A.D. 150 with the possible exception of Philemon and III John."[1]

- What's so great about that?

1. The above quotations from early Christians are significant because they help establish the trustworthiness of the New Testament. Some scholars have tried to discredit the fact that the New Testament was written in the first century by saying it is a second century fraud. However, the existence of quotations from the New Testament which date as early as 70 A.D. is positive evidence which refutes a second century hypothesis. After all, how could we have quotations from a book before it had been written?

2. One example of an early Christian source which sheds light on the trustworthiness of the New Testament is a religious handbook called the Didache. This book contains numerous New Testament quotations and had already been widely circulated throughout the Christian church by 150 A.D. The existence and wide circulation of this handbook is proof positive that the writing of the New Testament was completed by the end of the first century.

SKEPTICS ARE IMPRESSED

B. The above evidence along with a great deal more had, by the middle of the Twentieth Century convinced world renowned archaeologist W. F. Albright that the New Testament was written in the first century. This fact is even more impressive when we realize that Dr. Albright started out where many professors still are today—believing that the New Testament was a second century composition. But by 1955 Dr. Albright had been forced by the sheer weight of the evidence to radically change his views.

- Dr. Albright has asserted that "We can already say emphatically tha there is no longer any solid basis for dating any book of the New Testament after A.D. 80, two full generations before the date between 130 and 150 given by more radical New Testament critics of today."[2]

C. The following will give you a feel for the significance of early Christian quotations in establishing the authenticity of the New Testament.

QUESTION: Suppose that the New Testament had been destroyed by the third century. Could it have been collected together again from the writings of the early Christians?

ANSWER: One Christian scholar was asked that very question. Since he possessed all the existing writings of Christians from the second and third centuries he set out to see if he could reconstruct the New Testament from the quotations of early Christians. After months of research he responded to those who had asked him that question by saying that "**up to this time I have found the entire New Testament, except eleven verses.**"[3]

- More recently, New Testament scholar J. Harold Greenlee has said, "These quotations [early Christian quotations] are so extensive that the New Testament could virtually be reconstructed from them without the use of the New Testament Manuscripts."[4]

THEREFORE

If all the copies of the New Testament were destroyed, we could still reconstruct the text of the New Testament from quotations of early Christians.

III. NON-CHRISTIAN WRITINGS

- Have you ever heard someone say, "We can't really be sure that Jesus ever existed since the only place we hear of him is in the Bible"?

- We have already shown that there are numerous quotations outside the Bible from early Christians that refer to Jesus Christ, but how about non-Christian writings? Do they ever mention Jesus Christ?

SETTING THE SCENE

A. Before examining the non-Christian evidence for the reliability of the New Testament, it is important to understand the historical scene in which Christianity was born. Christianity was viewed by the Romans as just another religious cult that had sprung up in Palestine, a small insignificant land at the eastern corner of the vast Roman Empire.

B. When placing early Christianity in its historical perspective it is not surprising to find that the ancient secular historians wrote little about first century Christianity. However, if Jesus Christ did truly exist we would expect to find some secular references to this new religious leader. But do we?

C. To date we have found several references from secular historians regarding the life and teachings of Christ and his followers. In fact, these historians confirm rather than contradict the essential facts that are recorded in the New Testament. There are several non-Christian sources that substantiate the historicity of the New Testament. Such non-Christian historians as Tacitus, Lucian, Josephus, Seutonius, Thallus and many others allude to basic facts found in the Scriptures.

JESUS IN SECULAR HISTORY

1. A Jewish historian named Flavius Josephus who lived in the first century had this to say about Jesus. "Now there was about this time Jesus, a wise man, if it be lawful to call him a man, for he was a doer of wonderful works, a teacher of such men as receive the truth with pleasure. He drew over to him both many of the Jews, and many of the Gentiles. He was the Christ [Messiah], and when Pilate, at the suggestion of the principal men among us, had condemned him to the cross, those that loved him at the first did not forsake him; for he appeared to them alive again on the third day; as the divine prophets had foretold these and ten thousand other wonderful things concerning him. And the tribe of Christians so named from him are not extinct at this day."[5]

2. A Roman historian named Tacitus was born in 52 A.D. In his writings he makes reference to the death of Christ and of the existence of Christians at Rome. Tacitus even mentions Nero's vicious plan to blame the Christians for the fire at Rome. He says, "Hence to suppress the rumor, he falsely charged with the guilt, and punished with the most exquisite tortures, the persons commonly called Christians, who were hated for their enormities. Christus, the founder of the name, was put to death by Pontius Pilate, procurator of Judea in the reign of Tiberius: but the pernicious superstitution, repressed for a time broke out again, not only through Judea, where the mischief originated, but through the city of Rome also."[6]

3. Lucian, a second century Greek satirist, was extremely antagonistic to Christianity. However, his satirical wit has helped verify the essential facts of the life and teachings of Christ. He alludes to Christ as "the man who was crucified in Palestine because he introduced this new cult into the world." He again satirically makes reference to Christ when he says, "Furthermore, their first lawgiver persuaded them that they were all brothers one of another after they have transgressed once for all by denying the Greek gods and by worshipping that crucified sophist himself and living under his law."[7]

4. Thallus, a Gentile historian about 50 A.D., wrote about Christ and interestingly enough mentioned the darkness which fell upon the land during Christ's crucifixion. Even the Jewish Talmuds speak of the existence of Christ.[8]

CHRIST-A MAN OF HISTORY

Let's face it. Anyone who rejects the literal existence of Christ or His disciples simply hasn't read history. Non-Christian historians have verified the essential facts recorded in the Gospels. As Dr. F. F. Bruce has concluded, "Some writers may toy with the fancy of a 'Christ-myth,' but they do not do so on the ground of historical evidence. The historicity of Christ is as axiomatic [self-evident] for an unbiased historian as the historicity of Julius Caesar. It is not historians who propagate the 'Christ-myth' theories."[9]

IV. WHAT ABOUT ARCHAEOLOGY?

Has archaeology strengthened or weakened confidence in the reliability of the Bible?

A. Dr. Millar Burrows of Yale University has said that modern archaeology has "unquestionably strengthened confidence in the reliability of the Scriptural record. More than one archaeologist has found his respect for the Bible increased by the experience of excavation in Palestine."[10]

CRITICS GET CRITICIZED!

B. Dr. Burrows has also said, "Archaeology has in many cases refuted the views of the modern critics, It has shown in a number of instances that these views rest on false assumptions and unreal, artificial schemes of historical development."[11]

QUESTION: Has archaeology ever uncovered one mistake in the Bible?

ANSWER: Dr. Nelson Glueck, one of the leading Jewish archaeologists of our time, has said, "It may be stated categorically that no archaeological discovery has ever controverted [contradicted] a Biblical reference."[12]

> *"The excessive skepticism shown toward the Bible by important historical schools of the eighteenth and nineteenth centuries, certain phases of which still appear periodically, has been progressively discredited. Discovery after discovery has established the accuracy of innumerable details, and has brought increased recognition to the value of the Bible as a source of history."*[13]
>
> *–Dr. W. F. Albright*

C. The "excessive criticism" that Dr. Albright refers to can be illustrated through the greatest archaeologist of the nineteenth century. One author has described the life of this man in the following way: "Sir William Ramsay is regarded as one of the greatest archaeologists ever to have lived. He was trained in the German historical school of the mid-nineteenth century. As a result, he was taught that the Book of Acts was a product of the mid-second century A.D. He was firmly convinced of this belief and set out to prove this teaching. However, he was compelled to a complete reversal of his beliefs due to the overwhelming evidence uncovered in his research."[14]

FROM DOUBT TO FACT!

- After years of research, Sir William Ramsay wrote his conclusions in a book entitled, *The Bearing of Recent Discovery on the Trustworthiness of the New Testament.* He said, "Luke is a historian of the first rank; not merely are his statements of fact trustworthy; he is possessed of the true historic sense; . . . In short, this author should be placed along with the very greatest of historians."[15]

WHAT DOES THE FUTURE HOLD?

D. Archaeology has never contradicted one Biblical reference, but what about the future? Dr. Albright, who is one of the leading authorities on Biblical archaeology, believes that as time goes on, archaeology will continue to increase scholars' respect for the Bible. He predicts that, "As critical study of the Bible is more and more influenced by the rich new material from the ancient Near East we shall see a steady rise in respect for the historical significance of now neglected or despised passages and details in the Old and New Testament."[16]

V. THE VERDICT IS IN

- In the last four chapters we have placed the New Testament on trial. The witnesses have given their testimony. We have found that whether we listen to the bibliographic, internal or external witness, the conclusion is the same. Whether one goes to the New Testament documents themselves or surrounding literature or archaeology the verdict on the reliability of the New Testament is in. Almost forty years ago Sir Frederic Kenyon, former director and principal librarian of the British Museum, gave us the verdict. After years of detailed research, Kenyon concluded that, "the last foundation for any doubt that the Scriptures have come down to us substantially as they were written has now been removed. Both the authenticity and the general integrity of the books of the New Testament may be regarded as finally established."[17]

"No book from antiquity comes to the modern world with greater evidence for its authenticity than does the Bible. Both the kind and the amount of evidence that supports the fidelity of the present critical text are greater than for any other book from the ancient world."[18]

–Drs. Geisler and Nix

1. What is the latest possible date for dating the completion of the writing of the New Testament according to Dr. W. F. Albright?

____

2. List some of the early non-Christian historians who mention the existence of Jesus and His disciples.

____

____

3. Has archaeology strengthened or weakened confidence in the reliability of the Bible? How has it done so?

____

____

____

____

Footnotes

1. Norman L. Geisler and William E. Nix, *A General Introduction to the Bible,* Chicago: Moody Press, 1968, p. 350.

2. William F. Albright, *Recent Discoveries in Bible Lands,* New York: Funk and Wagnalls, 1955, p. 136.

3. Geisler, op. cit., p. 357.

4. Harold J. Greenlee, *Introduction to New Testament Textual Criticism,* Grand Rapids, Michigan: William B. Eerdmans Publishing Company, 1964, p. 54.

5. Josh McDowell, *Evidence That Demands a Verdict,* Arrowhead Springs, California: Campus Crusade for Christ, 1972, pp. 84-85.

6. Ibid., p. 84.

7. Ibid.

8. Ibid., p. 86.

9. F. F. Bruce, *The New Testament Documents: Are They Reliable?,* Downers Grove, Illinois: InterVarsity Press, 1964, p. 119.

10. Millar Burrows, *What Mean These Stones?,* New York: Meridian Books, 1956, p. 1.

11. Ibid., p. 291.

12. Nelson Glueck, *Rivers in the Desert: History of Neteg,* Philadelphia: Jewish Publications Society of America, 1969, p. 31.

13. William F. Albright, *The Archaeology of Palestine,* Rev. ed., Harmondsworth, Middlesex: Pelican Books, 1960, p. 127-128.

14. McDowell, op. cit., p. 72.

15. Sir William Ramsay, *The Bearing of Recent Discovery on the Trustworthiness of the New Testament,* London, Hodder and Stoughton, 1915, p. 222.

16. William F. Albright, *From the Stone Age to Christianity,* Baltimore: Johns Hopkins Press, 1946, p. 81.

17. Frederic G. Kenyon, *The Bible and Archaeology,* New York: Harper & Row, 1940, p. 288.

18. Geisler, op. cit., p. 447.

DIG DEEPER WITH THESE BOOKS

Geisler, Norman L. and William E. Nix. *A General Introduction to the Bible.* Chicago: Moody Press, 1968.

Little, Paul E. *Know Why You Believe.* Wheaton, Illinois: Scripture Press Publications, 1967.

McDowell, Josh. *Evidence That Demands a Verdict.* Arrowhead Springs, California: Campus Crusade for Christ, 1972.

McDowell, Josh. *More Than a Carpenter.* Wheaton, Illinois: Tyndale House Publishers, 1977.

Montgomery, John Warwick. *History and Christianity.* Downers Grove, Illinois: InterVarsity Press, 1964.

Pinnock, Clark H. *Set Forth Your Case.* Chicago: Moody Press, 1967.

Unger, Merril F. *Archaeology and the New Testament.* Grand Rapids: Zondervan Publishing House, 1962.

8/17

IS THE OLD TESTAMENT ANCIENT FABLE CR AMAZING FACT?

9 THE OLD TESTAMENT: IN THE FIERY FURNACE

In the previous chapters we put the New Testament on trial to determine whether it could be trusted. We discovered that it was extremely reliable and could not be ignored as a historical source.

But what about the Old Testament? It is even more ancient than the New. Could such an ancient document which had to be hand-copied hundreds of years longer than the New Testament be in any sense of the word trustworthy?

Many teachers and professors who teach high school and college Bible courses believe that the Old Testament is more fable than fact. Is the **information** from which these teachers draw their conclusions trustworthy?

It seems that those who reject the reliability of the Old Testament do it for two basic reasons. First, they have an anti-supernatural bias. That is, they **believe, by faith**, that miracles can't happen. This bias assumes that all miracles recorded in the Bible can either be explained by purely natural causes, or can be rejected as mere myth. They don't care how much historical evidence is available for a Biblical miracle, like the resurrection of Jesus Christ. They have already closed their minds to the possibility of God working in history (doing miracles). This attitude hardly seems open-minded and objective.

The second reason they reject the reliability of the Old Testament is lack of knowledge. Many teachers are unaware of the new evidence that's available for the trustworthiness of the Old Testament. Some have been fed a bill-of-goods by those who have been **their** teachers. Old Testament scholar Dr. R. Laird Harris has said, "We may conlude our rather technical study of the Old Testament text by saying that new evidence as well as older study gives us adequate grounds for saying that the sacred text of the Hebrew Old Testament is completely reliable."[1]

Can it really be demonstrated to a reasonable mind that the Old Testament is trustworthy? **Yes**, and that is what this next section is designed to do.

I. THE OLD TESTAMENT ON TRIAL

HAVE YOU EVER HEARD . . . ?

A. Oh, you can't trust the Old Testament. After all, it was copied in an age of ignorance by some half-literate, unsophisticated scribe that really didn't know what he was doing.

B. This objection only proves the ignorance of the objector. As Dr. William F. Albright, the leading 20th century archaeologist, has said, "The prolonged and intimate study of the many scores of thousands of pertinent documents from the ancient Near East proves that sacred [this includes the Old Testament] and profane documents were copied with greater care than is true of scribal copying in Graeco-Roman times."[2]

> *It is evident that the work of a scribe was a highly professional and carefully executed task . . . . Since he believed he was dealing with the Word of God, he was acutely aware of the need for extreme care and accuracy.*[3]
>
> *–Professor Paul E. Little*

II. EVALUATING THE RELIABILITY OF THE OLD TESTAMENT

- In evaluating the reliability of the Old Testament, one will find that it is just as reliable as the New, but for somewhat different reasons.

A. We learned earlier that the copies of the New Testament have a relatively large number of copyist errors which can be corrected by comparing and analyzing the abundance of existing New Testament copies (20,000). On the other hand, the Old Testament has few copyist errors and relatively few manuscript copies. In fact, until the discovery of the Dead Sea Scrolls in 1947, there were only a handful of Hebrew manuscripts in existence with the oldest dating back to around 900 A.D. This is about a thirteen-hundred year time gap between the completion of the Old Testament (400 B.C.) and the earliest existing copy (900 A.D.).

- The skeptic usually criticizes the reliability of the Old Testament by saying that it can't be reliable since we only have a handful of Old Testament copies which were copied hundreds of years after the original.

B. At first it may seem that the skeptic is right. But first impressions can be wrong. Actually, the existence of only a few Old Testament copies (until the discovery of the Dead Sea Scrolls) along with the fact that these copies are relatively modern in origin is strong evidence *in favor* of their reliability!

III. WHAT ABOUT THOSE ILLITERATE SCRIBES???

- The efficiency of the ancient Jewish scribes is one of the major reasons why we can trust the Old Testament Scriptures.

A. To see why the existence of only a few copies of the Old Testament is compelling evidence for their reliability we must first understand the true devotion and ability of ancient Jewish scribes. Far from being ignorant, untrained laymen, the scribes who copied the Scriptures were probably the most educated and literate people of the ancient world. For example, Ezra, an Old Testament scribe, was called "a scribe skilled in the law of Moses" (Ezra 7:6). These scribes would be like a combination of a modern-day lawyer and theologian.

THEY WERE DEAD SERIOUS

B. The scribes approached their job with complete dedication. They religiously and meticulously followed strict rules in copying the Old Testament. Since these scribes were convinced that they were copying the very Word of God they made sure the copies were exact duplicates of the original. Their devotion went to the point of giving their lives if need be. For example, if a king addressed them while they were copying the name of God, they were to ignore the king and his command. That could mean instant death!

"The fidelity [reliability] of the New Testament text depends upon the multiplicity of manuscripts; whereas, in the Old Testament, the accuracy of the text results from the ability and reliability of the scribes who transmitted it.[4]

—Norman L. Geisler, Ph.D.

C. The Old Testament was copied with this exactness right from the beginning. As the Old Testament was being written, it was immediately recognized by the author's contemporaries as the Word of God. For example, the Old Testament prophet Daniel quotes from a book written by one of his contemporaries, Jeremiah, as "the Word of the Lord" (Daniel 9:2). Not only was the Old Testament immediately recognized as the Word of God, but it was immediately copied with exactness. An Old Testament example of this can be found in the book of Jeremiah, chapter 36, where the scribe Baruch was commanded by Jeremiah to duplicate exactly a copy of the book he had written.

IV. WHY SO FEW OLD OLD TESTAMENT COPIES?

FIRST: Because the scribes would only accept exact copies of the Old Testament as being worthy of existence.

- To insure exactness, the scribes who copied the Old Testament followed strict rules. Some of these rules are listed by Dr. Samuel Davidson as follows:

"(1) A synagogue roll must be written on the skins of clean animals, (2) prepared for the particular use of the synagogue by a Jew. (3) These must be fastened together with strings taken from clean animals. (4) Every skin must contain a certain number of columns, equal throughout the entire codex. (5) The length of each column must not extend over less than 48 or more than 60 lines; and the breadth must consist of thirty letters. (6) The whole copy must be first-lined; and if three words be written without a line, it is worthless. (7) The ink should be black, neither red, green, nor any other color, and be prepared according to a definite recipe. (8) An authentic copy must be the exemplar, from which the transcriber ought not in the least deviate. (9) No word or letter, not even a yod, must be written from memory, the scribe not having looked at the codex [copy] before him . . . (10) Between every consonant the space of a hair or thread must intervene; (11) Between every new parashah, or section, the breadth of nine consonants; (12) between every book, three lines. (13) The fifth book of Moses must terminate exactly with a line, but the rest need not do so. (14) Besides this, the copyist must sit in full Jewish dress, (15) wash his whole body, (16) not begin to write the name of God with a pen newly dipped in ink, (17) and should a king address him while writing that name he must take no notice of him."[5]

- Dr. Davidson goes on to say that if these rules were not explicitly followed, the faulty copies "are condemned to be buried in the ground or burned; or they are to be banished to the schools, to be used as reading books."[6]

SECOND: Older manuscripts were looked at by the scribes as inferior to the newly copied manuscripts.

- Sir Frederic Kenyon gives a second reason for the scarcity of Old Testament copies when he says, "The same extreme care which was devoted to the transcription of manuscripts is also at the bottom of the disappearance of the earlier copies. When a manuscript had been copied with the exactitude prescribed by the Talmud, and had been duly verified, it was accepted as authentic and regarded as being of equal value with any other copy. If all were equally correct, *age gave no advantage to a manuscript*; on the contrary, age was a positive disadvantage, since a manuscript was liable to become defaced or damaged in the lapse of time. A damaged or imperfect copy was at once condemned as unfit for use . . . .

- Kenyon continues by saying, "Thus, far from regarding an older copy of the Scriptures as more valuable, the Jewish habit has been to prefer the newer, as being the most perfect and free from damage . . .

  "The absence of very old copies of the Hebrew Bible need not, therefore, either surprise or disquiet us."[7]

THIRD: The Jewish persecution that has taken place throughout history has resulted in the destruction of thousands of manuscripts.

- The history of the Jews is one of great persecution. It has driven them throughout all parts of the world. Their beloved city Jerusalem (ironically meaning city of peace) was conquered by outsiders 47 times between 1800 B.C. and 1948 A.D. Hatred for the Jews has caused many enemies to try to destroy Israel's beloved Scriptures.

FOURTH: Ancient copies were made on materials that were perishable.

- The Old Testament was copied and recopied for hundreds of years on various animal skins that would perish with time. Time and use would gradually deface a copied manuscript to the point that it would be discarded. Thus, the need arose for manuscripts to be copied and recopied. Considering all the forces working against the preservation of Old Testament manuscripts, it is a wonder that we have any at all!

FIFTH: The standardizing of the Hebrew Old Testament by Jewish scribes resulted in the destruction of many copies.

- Drs. Geisler and Nix give a final reason for the scarcity of Old Testament copies. This reason "dates back to the fifth and sixth centuries of our era, when the Masoretes (Jewish scribes) standardized the Hebrew text. It is believed that when their great work of vocalizing (putting in the vowel letters) and standardizing the Scriptures was completed, they systematically and completely disposed of all deviating manuscripts."[8]

THE FIRST TEXTUAL CRITICS

- Generally speaking, the Jewish scribes of the fifth and sixth centuries A.D. did what modern textual critics do today. They compared and analyzed manuscripts so they could establish the most exact text. After these scribes (called Masoretes) produced their "Masoretic Text," they destroyed all the imperfect manuscripts with the purpose of providing future generations with the most accurate text.

BUT ???

V. HOW ACCURATE IS THIS "MASORETIC TEXT"

- The "Masoretic Text" is our standard Hebrew Old Testament.

OLD TESTAMENT IS #1

A. Dr. William Henry Green, former professor of Old Testament literature at Princeton, has written, "It may be safely said that no other work of antiquity has been so accurately transmitted."[9]

B. In his discussion on the trustworthiness of the Masoretic text, Old Testament scholar Gleason Archer has concluded, "They . . . [Jewish scribes] gave the most diligent attention to accurate preservation of the Hebrew Scriptures that has ever been devoted to any ancient literature, secular or religious, in the history of human civilization."[10]

C. Drs. Geisler and Nix summarize several lines of evidence "which suggest that although the number of Masoretic manuscripts is small, their quality is very good."[11]

- They present such evidence as: (1) The reverence the Jewish scribes had for the Bible, (2) the very few variant readings, (3) comparison of duplicate passages in the Old Testament (for example, Psalm 4 and 53 are identical and are accurately transmitted in the Masoretic text), and (4) proof from archaeology.

- However, Geisler and Nix suggest that the best line of evidence comes from the Greek translation of the Old Testament known as the Septuagint. The Septuagint is the Greek translation of the Hebrew Old Testament (about 250 B.C.). When comparing this Greek translation, which was completed more than one thousand years before the Masoretic text (900 A.D.), we find the Septuagint "reflects an almost literal book-for-book, chapter-by-chapter translation of the Hebrew Scriptures as they are found in the Masoretic text, with the common stylistic and idiomatic differences."[12]

D. If the above were all the evidence we had, it would be enough to establish the reliability of the transmission of the Old Testament text. But with the discovery of the Dead Sea Scrolls in 1947 there is now additional and almost overwhelming evidence for the trustworthiness of our modern-day Old Testament. In our final chapter, we will discuss the importance of the Dead Sea Scrolls in establishing the amazing accuracy of the Old Testament.

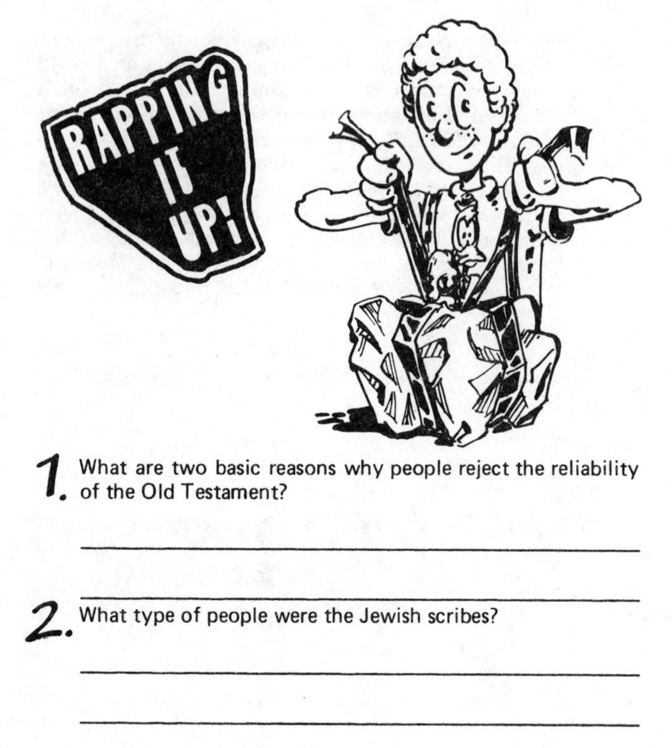

1. What are two basic reasons why people reject the reliability of the Old Testament?

____

____

2. What type of people were the Jewish scribes?

____

____

____

3. What are some of the reasons why, until the discovery of the Dead Sea Scrolls, there were so few Old Testament copies in existence?

____

____

____

____

Footnotes

1. R. Laird Harris, ed. by Howard F. Vos, *Can I Trust the Bible?,* Chicago: Moody Press, 1963, p. 132.

2. W. F. Albright, *From the Stone Age to Christianity,* Garden City, New York: Doubleday, Anchor Books, 1957, pp. 78-79.

3. Paul E. Little, *Know Why You Believe,* Wheaton, Illinois: Scripture Press Publications, 1967, p. 88.

4. Norman L. Geisler and William E. Nix, *A General Introduction to the Bible,* Chicago: Moody Press, 1968, p. 252.

5. Ibid., p. 241.

6. Josh McDowell, *Evidence That Demands a Verdict,* Arrowhead Springs, California: Campus Crusade for Christ, 1972, p. 57.

7. Frederic Kenyon, *Our Bible and the Ancient Manuscripts,* New York: Harper and Brothers, 1941, p. 43.

8. Geisler, op. cit., p. 251.

9. William Henry Green, *General Introduction to the Old Testament—The Text,* New York: C. Scribner's Sons, 1899, p. 181.

10. Gleason L. Archer, *A Survey of Old Testament Introduction,* Chicago: Moody Press, 1964, p. 65.

11. Geisler, op. cit., p. 252.

12. Ibid., p. 253.

10

THE OLD TESTAMENT:

THE SCROLLS THAT SHUT THE MOUTHS OF LIONS

The Dead Sea Scrolls brought new life and light to the question of whether the Old Testament was reliable. Before their discovery, many skeptics rejected the Old Testament's reliability because it had so few ancient copies. Now, however, with the discovery of the Dead Sea Scrolls, that objection is no longer valid.

I. THE DEAD SEA SCROLLS ARE ANYTHING BUT DEAD.

- What are the Dead Sea Scrolls?

A. The Dead Sea Scrolls are manuscripts made up of some 40,000 fragments of secular, religious and Biblical documents that date back to before the birth of Christ. They have been called "the greatest manuscript discovery of the century!"[1]

HOW WERE THEY FOUND?

B. Ironically, and in God's good timing, a shepherd boy in 1947 was looking for a lost sheep eight miles south of Jericho. He was just west of the Dead Sea when he tossed a stone into a hole of a cliff. This rock shattered a jar of pottery. As he investigated further he found large jars containing leather scrolls. It was later discovered that these jars had been left by a small Jewish sect called the "Qumran Community." This sect existed from 150 B.C. to 70 A.D.

C. This ancient community was dedicated to copying and preserving the Scriptures. As the Roman invasion of the Middle East grew closer, this sect realized that their Holy Scriptures were in danger of destruction and therefore hid their precious scrolls in caves near the Dead Sea. That is where the scrolls remained for 1900 years until a young shepherd boy *accidently* stumbled upon them in 1947.

II. WHAT'S THE BIG DEAL ABOUT THESE OLD SCROLLS?

A. The significance of this find in relation to our study is that among these manuscripts are found portions of every book of the Old Testament except Esther! Remember, before this find in 1947 the oldest copies of the Old Testament we possessed dated at 900 A.D. These Old Testament manuscripts that make up a portion of the Dead Sea Scrolls date as far back as the first and second century B.C.; about a thousand years earlier.

B. This monumental discovery gave us the opportunity again* to test the care and accuracy of the ancient Jewish scribes in copying the Old Testament. We could again refute the critics' skepticism of the reliability of the Old Testament by comparing the Masoretic text (900 A.D.) with the Dead Sea Scrolls (100 B.C.). As Professor Paul Little has said, "In one dramatic stroke, almost 1,000 years were hurdled in terms of the age of the manuscripts we now possess. By comparing the Dead Sea Scrolls with the Masoretic text, we would get a clear indication of the accuracy, or lack of it, of the transmission over the period of nearly a millenium."[2]

* "Again" because in the last chapter we compared the Septuagint (Greek Old Testament dated about 250 B.C.) with the Masoretic text and found the two were amazingly agreeable.

III. WHAT DID THE SCHOLARS FIND?

- Old Testament scholar R. Laird Harris demonstrates the accuracy of the Masoretic text when compared to the Dead Sea Scrolls by comparing Isaiah 53 of the Dead Sea Scrolls with the same chapter in the Masoretic text.

  A. Keeping in mind that there is a one-thousand-year time gap between the two copies, Dr. Harris says, "The [Dead Sea] text is extremely close to our M.T. [Masoretic text]. A comparison of Isaiah 53 shows that only seventeen letters differ from the M.T. Ten of these are mere differences of spelling like our 'honor' or 'honour,' and make no change at all in meaning. Four more are very minor differences, such as the presence of the conjunction which is often a matter of style. The other three letters are the Hebrew word for 'light' which is added after 'they shall see' in verse 11. Out of 166 words in this chapter only this one word is really in question and it does not at all change the sense of the passage." Dr. Harris goes on to say, "This is typical of the whole manuscript."[3] *One word* is in question after a thousand years of copying!

UNBELIEVABLE ACHIEVEMENT!

> *The comparison of these two texts "gives testimony to the* unbelievable achievement *of some scribes in faithfully preserving the text."*[4]
>
> *—Bruce Waltke, Ph.D.*

B. Gleason Archer has concurred with Harris and Waltke when he says that the Isaiah copies of the Dead Sea Scrolls "prove to be word for word identical with our standard Hebrew Bible in more than 95% of the text. The 5% of variation consisted chiefly of obvious slips of the pen and variations in spelling."[5]

WONDER OF WONDERS!

C. One of the leading authorities on the Dead Sea Scrolls is Millar Burrows of Yale University. He has written, "It is a matter for wonder that through something like a thousand years the text underwent so little alteration. As I said in my first article on the scroll, 'Herein lies its chief importance, supporting the fidelity of the Masoretic tradition.' "[6]

IV. THE VERDICT IS IN ON THE OLD TESTAMENT

A. As with the New Testament we have placed the Old Testament on trial. We have called in the witnesses: the ancient scribes, the Masoretic text, and those venerable old Dead Sea scrolls. They have each given their testimony and the verdict has been rendered. The question to be answered was asked by Sir Frederic Kenyon as long ago as 1939 (before the discovery of the Dead Sea Scrolls). He asked, "Does this Hebrew text which we call Masoretic . . . faithfully represent the Hebrew text as originally written by the authors of the Old Testament?"[7]

- Dr. Kenyon answers his own question by saying, "The Christian can take the whole Bible in his hand and say without fear or hesitation that he holds in it the true Word of God, handed down without essential loss from generation to generation throughout the centuries."[8]

If there were any doubts about Dr. Kenyon's conclusion before 1947, the discovery of the Dead Sea Scrolls has, as Geisler and Nix have said, "dismiss[ed] any remaining doubts about the fidelity of the Masoretic text by providing scholars with hundreds of manuscripts including almost every book of the Old Testament, which antedate the extant [existing] Masoretic manuscripts by a thousand years. The result of scholarly comparison reveals that the MT [Masoretic text] and the various text types of the Dead Sea manuscripts are substantially identical."[9]

> *"We may conclude . . . by saying that new evidence as well as older study gives us adequate grounds for saying that the sacred text of the Hebrew Old Testament is completely reliable."*[10]
>
> *—R. Laird Harris, Ph.D.*

1. What are the Dead Sea Scrolls and when were they found?

___

___

___

2. How much older are the Dead Sea Scrolls than the Masoretic text?

___

3. In comparing these two texts, how accurate were the scribes in preserving the original text over this one thousand year period? (Cite the example of Isaiah 53 in your answer).

___

___

___

___

1. Josh McDowell, *Evidence That Demands A Verdict,* Arrowhead Springs, California: Campus Crusade for Christ, 1972, p. 60.

2. Paul E. Little, *Know Why You Believe,* Wheaton, Illinois: Scripture Press Publications, 1967, p. 89.

3. R. Laird Harris, ed. by Howard F. Vos, *Can I Trust the Bible?,* Chicago: Moody Press, 1963, p. 124.

4. Bruce K. Waltke, *Biblical Criticism: Historical, Literary, and Textual,* Grand Rapids, Michigan: Zondervan Publishing House, 1978, p. 52.

5. Gleason L. Archer, *A Survey of Old Testament Introduction,* Chicago: Moody Press, 1964, p. 65.

6. Millar Burrows, *The Dead Sea Scrolls,* New York: Viking, 1955, p. 304.

7. Frederic Kenyon, *Our Bible and the Ancient Manuscripts,* New York: Harper and Brothers, 1941, p. 47.

8. Ibid., p. 23.

9. Norman L. Geisler and William E. Nix, *A General Introduction to the Bible,* Chicago: Moody Press, 1968, p. 266.

10. Harris, op. cit., p. 132.

DIG DEEPER WITH THESE BOOKS

Allis, Oswald T. *The Old Testament: Its Claims and Critics.* Nutley, New Jersey: Presbyterian and Reformed, 1972.

Geisler, Norman L. and William E. Nix. *A General Introduction to the Bible.* Chicago: Moody Press, 1968.

Harris, R. Laird. ed. by Howard F. Vos. *Can I Trust the Bible?* Chicago: Moody Press, 1963.

Merrill, Eugene H. *An Historical Survey of the Old Testament.* Grand Rapids, Michigan: Baker Book Company, 1976.

Morris, Henry M. *Many Infallible Proofs.* San Diego, California: Creation Life Publishers, 1974.

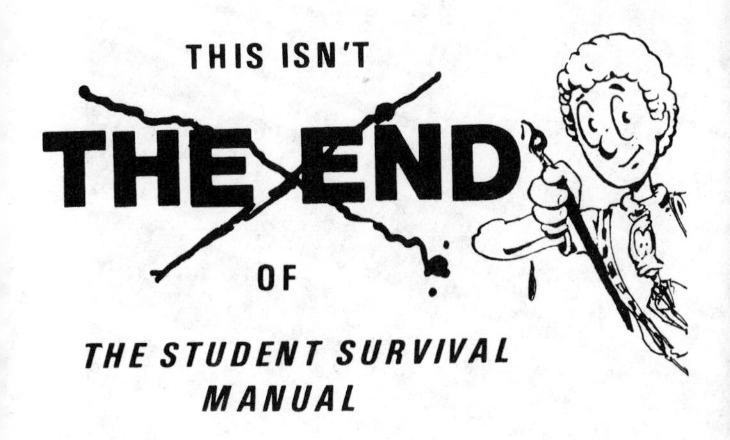

IT'S ONLY

THE BEGINNING

THE PEN IS STILL MIGHTIER THAN THE SWORD

"WITH THIS WE CONQUER"

When the Communists marched into Peking they carried banners with pictures of printing presses to proclaim the effectiveness of literature in conquering China.

A common saying in Africa is that, "The Christian missionaries taught Africans **how** to read, and the **Communists supply the reading material!"**

Who is supplying the reading material in your community? The **Caleb Campaign** is a nationwide effort to put Christian reading material into the hands of millions of American young people. Like Caleb of the Old Testament, you can rise up and conquer your part of the land with printed evidence for the Christian faith.

CALEB CAMPAIGN TOOLS

STUDENT ACTION FOR CHRIST
ISSUES & ANSWERS

S. A. C.
ISSUES & ANSWERS

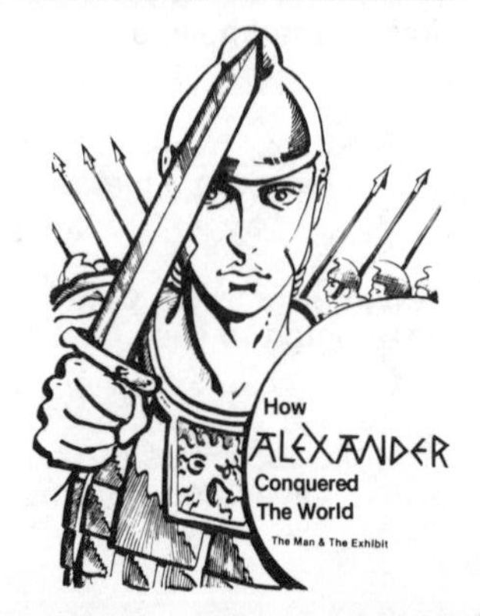

A BOOST FOR TEACHERS

THE CALEB CAMPAIGN

In a high school where the enrollment is dropping and teachers are being let go, Mr. Lane Anderson has seen the enrollment in his physics classes increase!

He says the scientific evidence for creation he gleans from **Issues & Answers** and **Active Christians In Education**, has made the course "come alive."

"Physics is more interesting now because I can show the application of God's laws. The laws of nature show that evolution is impossible. Many of my students are now creationists. They are debating other students trying to get them to re-examine their beliefs.

"Despite the drop in enrollment, I **added** a physics class this year. Using the newspaper has made me a better teacher, and has made the class better."

LANE ANDERSON --Park Ridge, Illinois

"Using the newspaper gives me an opportunity to let kids see that a teacher can talk about God and can present world history from a theistic viewpoint. When I read to the class Christopher Columbus' own words telling how the Holy Spirit had inspired him to sail to the Indies, it was as if an electric circuit had been connected in the room.

"Both publications give information about people in history or science that is not found in the textbooks.

"**Issues & Answers** takes a fresh look at social studies. I often use it as a reference for my class. It does the digging that I don't have time to do."

STEVE ADKINS --Sixth Grade Teacher West Frankfort, Illinois

TEACHER ADOPTION PLAN

Would you like to put these indispensable tools into the hands of teachers in your community? You can with the Teacher Adoption Plan! With your yearly donation, we'll mail these three valuable tools every month to anyone you choose:

ISSUES & ANSWERS HEROES OF HISTORY POSTERS
ACTIVE CHRISTIANS IN EDUCATION

TEACHERS RAISE FUNDS

"Eight teachers got together and raised the funds to adopt 135 teachers and school board members in our town.

"I wanted the other teachers to receive these newspapers because the Caleb Campaign has helped me as a teacher to see that I don't have to be afraid to mention God in the classroom.

"The theory of evolution is pushed hard in film strips and teaching materials. The other side is not given unless the teacher presents it. "Active Christians In Education," and "Issues & Answers" give the facts of the creation model and explain how to present them in class."

BOB MARAGNI
--Fifth Grade Teacher West Frankfort, Illinois

ACTIVE CHRISTIANS IN EDUCATION

ACTIVE CHRISTIANS IN EDUCATION (ACE) is a monthly newspaper to encourage the teaching of Christian perspectives in the public school.

Regular Features Include:
Interviews With Christian Teachers
Textbooks & Film Reviews
Teacher's Tips In History, Science, Literature, Etc.
Current Legal Rights

HEROES OF HISTORY POSTERS

Washington, Lincoln, Columbus, Newton, and many others come to life on 11" x 17" posters on parchtone paper. Each contains a pen and ink portrait of the hero and their Christian testimony in their own words.

FREE SAMPLE
Write to the address below and we'll send you a free sample of **Issues & Answers.**

SINGLE SUBSCRIPTION
For any donation to The Caleb Campaign we'll send you a full year of **Issues & Answers** and **Active Christians In Education (ACE).** Your contribution will help us reach many others.

BULK RATES
Issues & Answers is available in bundles of 15, 100, 250, or more. Please write for costs.

TEACHER ADOPTION PLAN
We'll send **Issues & Answers, ACE,** and a Hero of History Poster for a full year. Please write for cost.

CALEB CAMPAIGN TRAINING
Complete training is available for anyone wishing to become a Caleb Campaign Chairman. You'll learn how to distribute newspapers in order to reach 80 per cent of the students on any campus.

WRITE or **CALL**

THE CALEB CAMPAIGN / P.O.Box 608 / HERRIN, ILLINOIS 62948
Phone: [618] 942-7520

Ask for Dan Rodden, National Caleb Campaign Chairman

Please make check payable to THE CALEB CAMPAIGN, **AND INCLUDE YOUR COMPLETE NAME, ADDRESS, AND ZIP CODE.**

Recommended further reading:

If you enjoyed this book, we suggest that you order one or more of the following titles. You can order these books by sending a check directly to: **Mott Media, 1000 East Huron, Milford, MI 48042,** (Include 6% for postage and handling.)

Four Trojan Horses of Humanism, by Harry Conn. The author shares his thoughts and opinions with those who dare to think. True Christianity is worth dying for, but this will not be perceived until it (Christianity) has been purged of cheap grace, easy believism, and humanistic motives brought in by the theological Trojan Horse.
Paper, 122 pages **$5.95**

The Separation Illusion, by John Whitehead. Refutes the commonly-held belief that religion must be separated from government and applies this discussion to the court decisions on prayer and Bible reading in public schools. Paper, 210 pages, **$4.50**

Are Textbooks Harming Your Children? by James Hefley. Shocking quotes of the materials discovered by the Gablers in their reviews of public school texts. Informative information is given on how you, parents like themselves, can take action to improve American Education. Paper, 223 pages, **$4.25**

How to Tutor, by Samuel L. Blumenfeld. The book is divided into four parts: how to qualify as a tutor, reading primer, writing primer, and arithmetic primer. Useful for tutoring children sents concisely many ways to identify the blessings of God in your educational ministry. You will be blessed each time you meditate through the book. Paper, 111 pages, **$2.95**

Teacher's Report Card, by Mary Vandermey. A collection of short, warming and insightful vignettes about children and real teachers. Each chapter provides the reader with encouragement and inspiration from the Scriptures. Paper, 146 pages, $2.50 **NOW $1.00**

Bible Calculator Word Games, By Bennie Rhodes. A collection of fictious stories based on Bible names and characters which are arithmetic problems designed for use with a pocket calculator. For children ages 9-12, it is excellent for extra-time classroom use. Paper, 160 pages, **$2.95**

FACS - Fundamentals for American Christians, by Russ Walton, Basic Biblical principles of government that should be fundamentals for American Christians. Paper, 372 pages, **NOW $3.50**

The Sower Series of World Heroes
Character-building Christian Biographies
for Young Readers:

Christopher Columbus, by Bennie Rhodes. An exciting book about a Christian explorer who sought to discover new lands to spread the gospel at the risk of shipwreck, disease, and personal failure.
Cloth, $6.95; paper, $4.25

Robert E. Lee, by Lee Roddy. A Christian of impeccable character, Lee became one of the at the preschool level as a preventive measure during the first two grades of public school as a supplement to the child's instruction, or for use in remedial instruction at any grade level. Paper, 298 pages, $4.95 **NOW $1.50**

A Christian Approach to Education, by H.W. Bryne. An outstanding survey of the basic theories of Christian education. This is a new approach based on Biblical principles and compares the secular and Christian views of education prevalent today. Paper, 378 pages, $7.95 **NOW $6.95**

Asking Questions: A Classroom Model for Teaching the Bible, by D. Bruce Lockerbie. Each question leads to a variety of responses intended to teach, first, what the text says; then, what it means; and finally how its principles apply to Bible readers today. Paper, 157 pages, **$4.95**

Handbook on Athletic Perfection, by Wes Neal. "The perfect athletic performance can only be experienced by the Christian athlete controlled by the Holy Spirit who has been sent by God to develop Jesus Christ's attitudes and actions in your athletic performance as well as your entire life." Biblical premise for every principle stated and practical applications of those principles. Paper, 226 pages, **$5.95**

Handbook on Coaching Perfection, by Wes Neal. Thesis is "use me Lord to draw recognition back to you." Emphasis is on seeking what Scripture says and then doing things (even coaching) God's way. Excellent gift for coaches, athletes. Paper, 238 pages, **$5.95**

Teach Them Diligently, A Devotional Guide for Teachers Who Care, by Arthur Nazigian. Pre-